Praise for *Praying with Sacred Art*

"I am happy to recommend this work of aesthetic evangelization, authored by Derek Rotty, a lay leader in the Catholic Diocese of Memphis. In *Praying with Sacred Art,* Rotty uses the same kind of genius seen in our praying through the Joyful, Luminous, Sorrowful, and Glorious Mysteries of Christ the Lord. Rotty offers classic examples of sacred art, adding short meditations with each depiction, as he strives to assist the reader in this visio divina. He highlights the mysteries of Christ the Lord, arranging for visual prayer sacred art that speaks to the mysteries experienced in liturgical seasons. In inviting the reader to ponder the mysteries of Christ through this visual aesthetic, he has given us another help in our longing for the One who is both immanent and transcendent."

—***Bishop David P. Talley,*** Diocese of Memphis

"Derek Rotty's *Praying with Sacred Art* should be on every Catholic's bookshelf! This beautiful collection of art for *visio divina* provides the reader with well-organized and reflective meditations for every season of the liturgical year. Rotty connects divine art and his rich reflections on it in a way that enhances both and leads the reader to a deeper, more profound understanding of his own spiritual journey to the divine. A wonderful visual prayer book!"

—***Stephen Auth,*** Author, *Visions of the Divine*

"In *Praying with Sacred Art*, Derek Rotty escorts the reader into the mysteries of salvation through meditation and reflections on religious truths and scriptural events, as presented in the reveries of artists from all periods. Rotty does not belabor old details but offers new visions. This book would be a welcome addition to any library—and a particular plus to places of quiet thought and prayer—and as reading material for an afternoon spent in any art museum."

—***Dr. Geraldine M. Rohling,*** Archivist-Curator Emerita, Basilica of the National Shrine of the Immaculate Conception

"The beauty of Derek Rotty's book *Praying with Sacred Art* lies not only in his profound (and pertinent) meditations but also in the remarkable catholicity of his artistic selections. Through exquisite, expressive, and engaging paintings, drawn from more than a millennium of artistic traditions, Rotty presents old favorites in a new light and, as an added service, introduces new treasures by lesser-known masters. *Praying with Sacred Art* expands the reader's artistic lexicon while enhancing our *visio divina*."

—***Elizabeth Lev,*** Art Historian and Author, *How Catholic Art Saved the Faith*

"Great works of religious art can help the wandering mind focus on prayer. The distracted soul will find much to meditate on in this richly curated collection of beautiful works, paired with insightful commentary by Derek Rotty. I can imagine, especially, a world opening up for young people as they pore over the offerings of *Praying with Sacred Art.*"

—***Leila Lawler,*** Author, *The Summa Domestica*

"I've waited for a book like this for years. In these pages, Derek Rotty allows sacred art to do what it does best—slow us down, open our eyes, and draw us into the mysteries of Christ. As you move through the liturgical year and the life of Jesus, each meditation will make you feel as if you are standing before a holy image and hearing a quiet word meant only for you. These are not pages to rush through; they are holy pauses—in which beauty guides the soul toward the heart of God."

—***Elizabeth Zelasko,*** Sacred artist; Speaker; Author

PRAYING WITH SACRED ART

Derek Rotty

PRAYING WITH SACRED ART

Pondering the Mystery of Redemption through *Visio Divina*

SOPHIA INSTITUTE PRESS
Manchester, New Hampshire

Cover design by Enrique J. Aguilar

For cover and interior art please see image credits at the back of the book.

Sophia Institute Press
Box 5284, Manchester, NH 03108
1-800-888-9344
www.SophiaInstitute.com

Sophia Institute Press is a registered trademark of Sophia Institute.

paperback ISBN 979-8-88911-222-8

ebook ISBN 979-8-88911-223-5

Library of Congress Control Number: 2025943733

First printing

Contents

PART III
The Art of Lent & Holy Week

PART IV
The Art of Easter

PART V
The Art of Jesus' Public Ministry

PART VI
The Art of Jesus' Parables & Miracles

PRAYING WITH SACRED ART

Introduction

Pope Benedict XVI reminded the whole Church that its greatest priority in our modern world is "to enable the people of our time once more to encounter God, the God who speaks to us and shares his love so that we might have life in abundance." Every person ought to have an invitation; and the faithful must always encounter Jesus Christ anew, personally and communally, at every moment of their lives. Such an encounter is a thing of "immense beauty," wrote the Holy Father.[1] This book has been inspired by a series of ongoing encounters with the One who is Transcendent Beauty, and I offer it as a way for others to encounter the same Beauty.

To foster this necessary and beautiful encounter, we must believe that God continues to speak. If we believe *that* He speaks, we must also understand *how* He speaks and shares His love so we may have abundant life. Catholics believe there are four ways God speaks to each of us.

[1] Benedict XVI, apostolic exhortation *Verbum Domini* (September 30, 2010), no. 2.

The first two ways are necessary and rich sources of hearing the Word of God, but they are beyond the scope of this book. First, God speaks through His Church, the Mystical Body of Christ on earth. Before His Ascension, Jesus commissioned His apostles with the authority to use His own voice (see Luke 10:16; John 20:21–23); and this authority has been handed down through the centuries by apostolic succession. God also speaks through the Scriptures. The Sacred Page guides readers through the story of God's faithful covenant love, which culminates in His Incarnate Word, Jesus (see Heb. 1:1–2; 4:12).[2] These first two ways in which God speaks are certainly important for measuring the next two ways (see *Catechism of the Catholic Church* 748–795, especially 772, 787–789, and 795).

The last two ways in which God speaks are directly related to this book, and they provide much rich source material for meditation. First, God speaks to us through our desires, and even through our passions. The basic desire of every human heart is an enduring state of peace and contentment, also called beatitude. And our passions are emotions and inclinations that can help us achieve beatitude, if they are harnessed and ordered rightly. All emotions, especially fears and sufferings, can lead us into deeper union with Jesus, who has experienced all those same temptations and accomplished victory (see Heb. 4:15). The feelings and emotions we experience serve as a passageway, a conduit to and from the interior life of our mind and heart (see CCC 1718–1721, 1762–1770).

[2] To deepen one's devotion to the Word of God in Sacred Scripture, I recommend my book *A Life of Conversion: Meeting Christ in the Gospels* (Huntington, IN: Our Sunday Visitor, 2019).

Finally, God speaks through beauty, which touches our senses and captivates our hearts. Here, I rely on the classical definition of beauty, made clearest in the thought of St. Thomas Aquinas: beauty consists in *integritas* (wholeness), *consonantia* (proportionality), and *claritas* (radiance). A thing is beautiful if it coheres and will not fall apart, if it is balanced and fits well together, and if it shines forth a proverbial light that transcends itself. Beautiful things include sunsets, gardens, waterfalls, Gothic architecture, libraries, diligent scientific experiments, and the human person rightly understood.

Our Catholic Faith also reminds us that human persons have the ability to express their relationship with God and bring more beauty into the world through artistic work. Sacred art is "a freely given superabundance of the human being's inner riches." Art arises from God-given talent and skill, and it seeks to provide access to a higher and deeper reality "in a language accessible to sight or hearing" (CCC 2501; see also CCC 2502). This book is the result of one person reflecting at length on that superabundance gifted by talented artists across the centuries.

Still, all this theoretical information ought to lead us to some practical action. Thus, I offer this book and the practice of *visio divina*. The Latin term literally means "divine vision," but it effectively means "praying with sacred art." Its essence is a human person's effort to gaze into the divine. Praying with sacred art allows us to use our eyes differently. It allows us to gaze upon beauty so that the windows into our souls might let in the truly good light provided by the Holy Spirit (see Luke 11:33–36). We ought to gaze upon beauty, including sacred art, and realize how it stirs our souls to change and become more fully what and who God intends us to be.

Practically, then, this book offers a series of essays, each focused on a single great work of sacred art from the Christian tradition. Easily, there could have been other forms of art included, such as sculpture, but I have chosen only paintings as the fodder for meditation, simply because of the two-dimensional format of a book. There could have been untold numbers of additional essays based on other paintings. Those will be ripe for readers to continue pondering for many lifetimes.

The essays here printed are not intended to provide intricate lessons on artistic technique or sweeping lessons on art history. Scant lessons on those details are included when necessary or helpful. The primary objective of each essay is to allow the piece of art to serve as a window into the viewer's soul. How does the painting allow each person to connect more deeply with the Lord? Do the details of the painting elicit memories or emotions that lead us deeper into meditation? How might each viewer be inspired to act, based on the truth conveyed by the art?

More specifically, the essays are sorted into four basic sections. Since the mystery of redemption unfolds throughout the Church's liturgical year, we begin with a series of reflections on the art of Advent and Christmas. At the center of the liturgical year, and at the center of our redemptive process, are Lent, Holy Week, and Easter. These two sections are followed by a brief series reflecting on Jesus' childhood and quiet years in Nazareth. Finally, there is a longer series, far from complete and exhaustive, that provides an opportunity to meditate on Jesus' public ministry of exorcisms, miracles, and parables. All of these essays then culminate in a meditation on the terminus of our redemptory process.

This book is the result of my own *visio divina*, my own practice of gazing on art and prayerfully asking God to change my soul through the window of my sight. I pray that my reflections, and the process of transformation that has happened in me, will be of some benefit for those who read. I pray that all of us will be able, led by God's grace, to cultivate lives of integrity, proportion, and radiance.

This book is dedicated to the memory of Fr. Bill Parham, a dear friend, mentor, and pastor who loved to paint the mysteries of God on canvas and in the hearts of his parishioners. Fr. Bill had an indescribable and priceless influence on my own formation, my own ability to appreciate sacred art and understand the mystery of redemption. May his soul, and the souls of all the faithful departed, rest in peace.

PART I

The Art of Advent

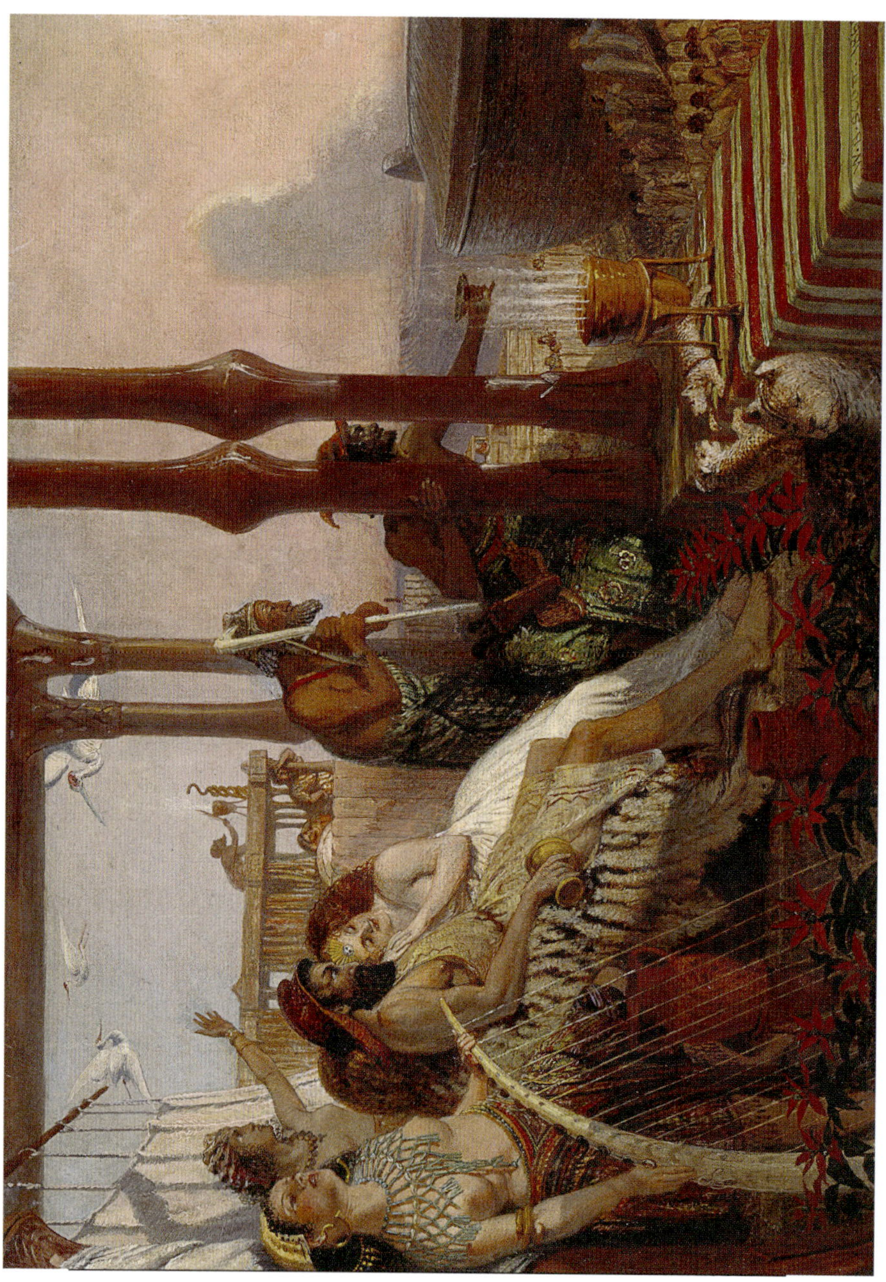

I

The Eve of the Deluge

At the beginning of the Advent season, the Church calls us to evaluate our lives and our stance before God so that we are ready for the Parousia (the Second Coming of Christ) and the Final Judgment. That's why each year the Gospel for the first Sunday of Advent warns us to be vigilant, to stay awake, and to prepare ourselves (see Matt. 24:37–44; Mark 13:33–37; Luke 21:25–28, 34–36). The Gospel reading for Year A of the Church's liturgical calendar presents Jesus' teaching about "the days of Noah" and the necessity of being prepared for the "coming of the Son of Man … at an hour you do not expect." In response to this reality, Jesus' startling exhortation is, "Therefore, stay awake!" (Matt. 24:37–44). Jesus' teaching was clearly meant to address the decadence that has been present in every age of human history, including His and ours. Guarding against such decadence, even overcoming it when it is present, is perhaps the most important effort that we can make during Advent, or any liturgical season.

The Eve of the Deluge, painted in 1865 by William Bell Scott, depicts quite well the contrast between the faithfulness and decadence in "the days of Noah" that Jesus mentioned. Scott draws us into the moment when the biblical patriarch made a very countercultural decision to build and enter an ark in preparation for a flood that seemed nowhere nigh but had been promised by a relatively unknown God. While the historical setting is the ancient Near East, we must be aware that the moral setting might be our own bodies, minds, and souls. We must be aware that we might be living in "the days of Noah" as much as that generation.

At the middle-left of the painting, a kingly figure reclines on a chair covered with tiger skin, embraces a young woman who is only half-covered by a sheet, and holds an empty chalice. Around this king are multiple other symbols of decadence: cheetahs, considered an unclean animal in the Mosaic Law; red lilies, signifying the human passions; and multiple bare-chested, intoxicated women, one of whom has been playing music. The whole scene bears the imprint of sensuality. As he sits in this position, the king glares with disdain out over the balcony, smugly looking at the ark and its inhabitants. Immediately, the viewer feels quite acutely the dichotomy of this historical moment: placation of the senses in contrast to the faithfulness that leads to ridicule and social disdain.

Near the king, directly in the middle of the painting, are two men who are certainly priests of the local pagan religion. The elder priest looks out with sleepy puzzlement, while the younger priest with a more sinister face engages in some form of incense ritual. In the background, in another area of the royal palace, a shadowy figure also prays with incense next to a sculpted bronze snake. What are they worshiping? For what do they pray in these "days of Noah"? The effect of this scene, as the effect of the Gospel passage, is to get viewers to ask if something has taken the place of the One, True God as the object of our worship.

Near the top of the painting, above the palace veranda, storks circle in the sky. These birds are probably placed in the scene as a direct reference to a prophecy spoken by Jeremiah when he tried to warn Israel of their impending spiritual death by exile. "Even the stork in the sky knows its seasons," Jeremiah exclaimed, "but my people do not know the order of the Lord" (8:7). Since that time, the stork has been symbolic of the fate of an unfaithful people. Thus, storks can be a great reminder to us during Advent that we ought to guard against obstinance to God's desires and commands.

On the right of the image is a red sky with a developing storm cloud. This might cause the viewer to recall Jesus' words about red skies earlier in the Gospel: "You know how to judge the appearance of the sky, but you cannot judge the signs of the times" (Matt. 16:2–3). Anyone trying to live faithfully in decadent times needs to ask the Lord if there is any moral deluge coming into my life that would separate me from the Lord. If so, how will I prepare and overcome it, even if it is not socially acceptable?

Below the cloud is the ark that Noah and his sons constructed. When we see the ark, we ought to see it as the vessel that provides shelter from the storm and allows God's covenant to move forward to the next generation. Throughout every generation since Noah, God's Chosen People, culminating in the Church, has been this vessel. This painting reminds us that in times of cultural decadence, as well as in times of personal difficulty, we can seek refuge in the Church rather than drown in our own troubles or the world's decadence.

Near the entrance of the ark are two groups of people, both of which are fairly indistinct. Eight people are entering the ark, those who were faithful to God's command. Other local citizens stand in a semicircle and watch. Perhaps they are questioning. Perhaps they are ridiculing. In any case, they are part of the culture that cannot see the value of preparing and entering the ark. The fact that both of these groups are less clearly drawn creates a great question for Advent: Am I living faithfully according to God's commands, even if I don't understand and even if I become a social pariah? Or do I stand by skeptically and cynically as others try to live faithfully? Do I judge others who have tried to read the signs of the times and act accordingly?

Just like the Gospel readings for the first week of Advent, Scott's painting draws us in to the perpetual problems of complacency and sloth. These were problems in "the days of Noah," they certainly are problems in our world today, and they definitely can encroach in our own lives. Viewing this painting provides a fantastic reminder that any one of us can slide slowly out of right relationship with God if we get caught up in the decadence of our culture. It also serves to remind us that God's judgment might be imminent at any time. Perhaps most importantly, *The Eve of the Deluge*, like Jesus' words in the Gospel, ultimately helps each of us to prepare for the coming of the Lord and our individual judgment. Our judgment could mean that we are carried away by a deluge of self-love, or it could mean that we are welcomed into the Eternal Ark of Heaven.

Therefore, each of us will do well to ponder *The Eve of the Deluge* this Advent. Let's hope it causes us to examine our lives for tendencies of complacency, decadence, and self-love so that we may become more like Noah and less like the decadent culture around us, and so that this Advent may be a productive and fruitful season in our lives.

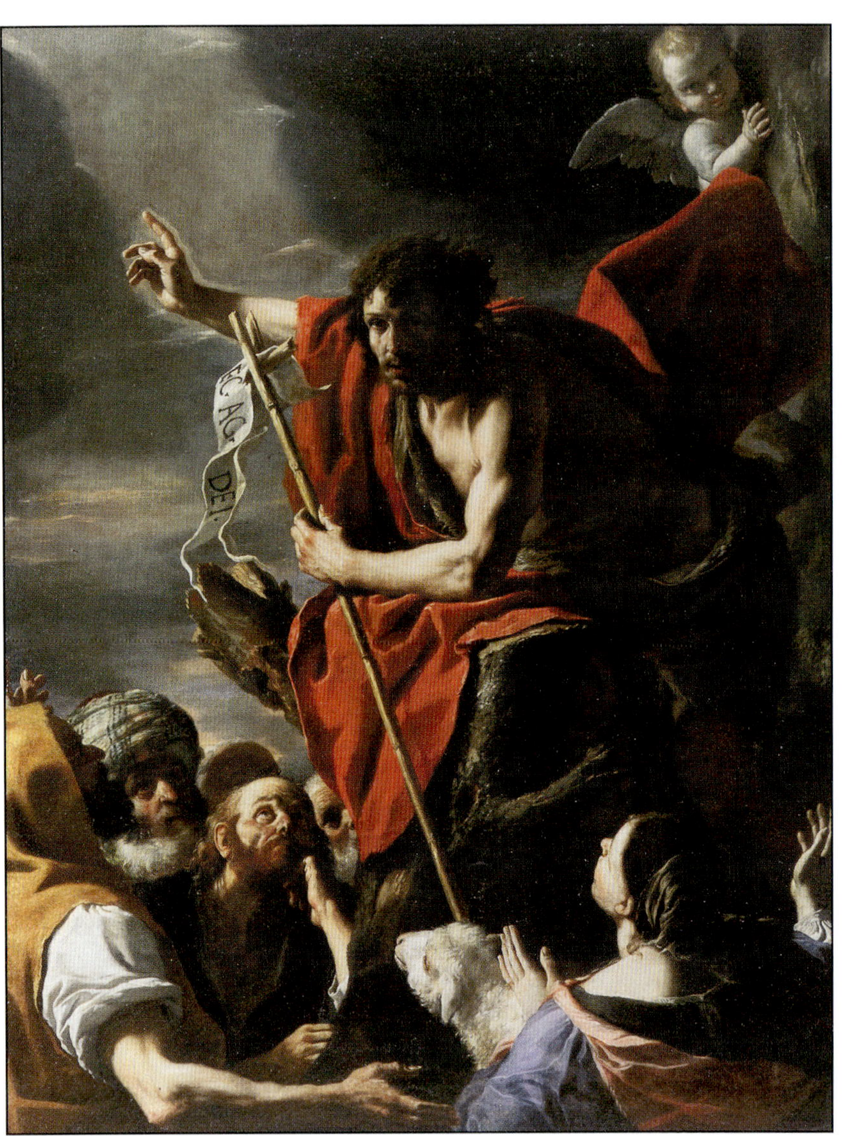
EC AG
DEI

2

St. John the Baptist Preaching

In the Gospel reading for the Second Week of Advent, we are introduced to John the Baptist (see Matt. 3:1–12; Mark 1:1–8; Luke 3:1–6). In the reading for Year A of the Church's liturgical calendar, we hear details of his wardrobe, his diet, and his ministry at the Jordan River, all of which are meant to recall the ministry of Elijah in the Old Testament. We also hear his exhortations for the Pharisees and Sadducees to "bear good fruit" through repentance and his warning for failure to do so. Finally, we hear the first description of "the one who is coming after me," the one who will "baptize you with the Holy Spirit and fire." This Mighty One coming after John will command repentance; He will cut down metaphorical trees at their very roots; and He will save good wheat while sending the chaff into "unquenchable fire" (Matt. 3:1–12). This entire scene causes us to recognize that Jesus and His Good News are not timid realities; they will require radical decisions and actions.

This riveting episode is captured in *St. John the Baptist Preaching*, painted by Mattia Preti in the 1660s.[3] Preti included elements drawn from each of the four Gospel accounts, details that call each and every viewer into the ministry and message of the voice "crying out in the desert." It is clear, in the moment of this painting, that the Baptist has already made the radical decisions and actions incumbent upon a follower of Jesus, and that he is passionately calling others to the same. Thus, during Advent, this painting provides a great opportunity for reflection on key decision points in our spiritual lives.

At first glance, we notice the dark, ominous sky in the background. On one hand, this sky signifies the tension that existed between John and the religious establishment, the "brood of vipers," as he called them (Matt. 3:7). On the other hand, it signifies the impending judgment for those who would not heed the message of repentance. Both of these angles are good to ponder during Advent. Am I falling into patterns of complacency and presumption as the Pharisees and Sadducees may have done? Am I open to repentance and conversion? Am I ready, willing, and able to bear the "good fruit" that is evidence of my repentance?

Next, we notice a large shaft of light piercing through the impending darkness. Almost certainly, this light is intended to cause viewers to call to mind the words of St. John the Evangelist: "The light shines in the darkness, and the darkness has not overcome it" (John 1:5). Even the Baptist's hand points up into the light and is illuminated by it. This detail

3 *St. John the Baptist Preaching*, by Mattia Preti, can be found at the San Francisco Museum of Fine Arts, California.

illustrates the very simple point of John the Baptist's message: the Light of the World has pierced the darkness of our fallen, sinful condition and has given us the opportunity to return to right relationship with God the Father. Advent allows us time to prepare our hearts to receive that reality in its fullness, and it offers us an opportunity to change if conversion is necessary.

This contrast between light and dark spreads into the center of the painting and causes us to focus on the Baptist. The question for each of us, the question of Advent, is whether or not we are willing and able to turn more fully toward the light that God desires to give us, the Light of the World to which John points us. This very idea becomes even more poignant as we notice John's gaze. John stares out toward the viewer, beyond the scope of this painting. It seems as though he is asking the viewer if she is willing to listen to his proclamation, to heed his call to repentance and conversion. This Advent, will I heed John's call? Will I refuse to presume my own righteousness? Will I bear the good fruit of justice, mercy, and faith? Will I recognize that the Kingdom of Heaven is near?

Just over John's left shoulder, from the upper-right corner of the painting, an angel also gazes out at the viewer. The angel is probably included because of St. Luke's version of this biblical event, which tells us that "the word of God came to John the son of Zechariah in the desert" (Luke 3:2). The title *angel* literally means "God's messenger," so the word of the Lord coming to John in the desert would have been brought by an angel. By his gaze, this angel also invites us to listen to John's message.

St. John was portrayed by Preti as a muscular man cloaked in a red garment. St. John's physical fitness surely would have been the result of his austere conditions and diet, and the red garment signifies his impending martyrdom. Both of these details can help us meditate in Advent. We ought to remember that every Christian disciple is called to an austerity of life, an austerity that will make us morally and spiritually strong, even if not physically so. John's red cloak causes us to remember that true prophets always bear some kind of martyrdom, either physical or social. During Advent, our Catholic Faith proposes the life and ministry of John the Baptist because we need to be preparing our bodies, minds, and spirits to be prophets in our own time, despite the martyrdom that will surely come our way.

To what or whom did St. John point in his ministry? To what or whom shall I point? The answer is obvious in the painting. John holds a staff, which evokes the authority of the first great prophets to Israel, Elijah and Elisha. The staff is in the shape of a cross and bears a banner with the Latin words *Ecce Agnus Dei* ("Behold the Lamb of God"). Beyond those two details, Preti placed the staff on a linear trajectory with the light coming out of Heaven, and it ends precisely at the lamb at the bottom of the painting. Of course, all of these elements point us toward Jesus, "the Lamb of God, who takes away the sin of the world" (John 1:29).

Perhaps the most intriguing detail might be missed if we don't look closely enough. John's red garment covers the stump of a tree, a tree that has borne the brunt of an axe. Without a doubt, this is significant of "every tree that does not bear good fruit," whose metaphorical fate John predicted (Matt. 7:19). During Advent, it is right for each of us to ask whether the fate of the tree will be our own, or whether we are ready to turn more fully to the Lord and produce the good fruit of repentance.

Finally, in the bottom third of the painting, a half-dozen people look up at the preacher. Several of them are in quizzical positions, while at least one looks a bit scared. One of the figures stands in a posture of wonderment, his head propped up by his fist. It seems that this man is in prayer, longing for the reality to which John points. As I gaze upon the painting, I can imagine myself in this audience. I must ask which of these figures represents me. Am I puzzled by the Gospel and its demands for my life? Am I prayerfully ready to receive John's message?

Preti's iconic painting offers us an opportunity for this Second Week of Advent to respond to St. John the Baptist, who wants to point us directly to Jesus Christ. It invites us to commit wholeheartedly to the life of discipleship, which will require radical choices and actions. Most importantly, it will help us to behold the Lamb of God and enter into a deeper relationship with Him.

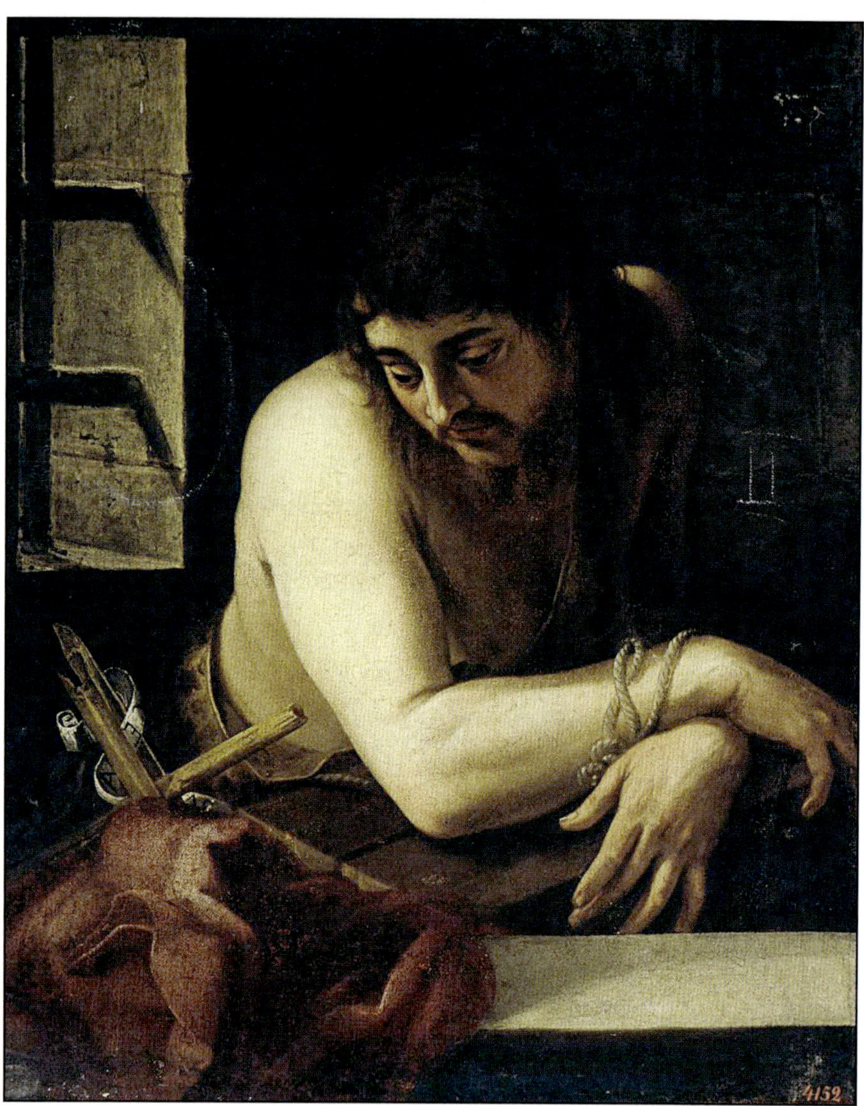
4152

3

St. John the Baptist in Prison

THE GOSPEL PASSAGES for the Third Sunday of Advent likewise tell of the ministry of St. John the Baptist (see Matt. 11:2–11; John 1:6–8, 19–28; Luke 3:10–18). The reading for Year A of the Church's liturgical calendar takes us to the last days of his life. When the scene begins, the "voice crying out in the desert" (John 1:23) finds himself sitting in a prison cell because he has ruffled the feathers of the religious and political establishment. The biblical passage tells us that John heard of the works that Jesus was doing around Galilee and Judea, so he sent his disciples to ask if Jesus was the hoped-for Messiah of Israel. Jesus' reply to John's disciples is basically, "Go and tell John that it should be obvious by the works that I do. These works are the fulfillment of the prophecy he spoke." Jesus turns to the crowd and announces that John was the messenger who had gone before to prepare the way before His own ministry of reconciliation and salvation. Jesus concludes by telling the crowd that John the Baptist is the greatest of all those born among women, but that "the least in the kingdom of heaven is greater than he" (Matt. 11:11).

This Gospel passage offers every hearer the opportunity to reflect on the zeal with which John the Baptist began his ministry, as well as the potential despair of his later condition. We can be certain that John would have wondered, while sitting in his cell, if all of his work had been inspired by the Lord at all, or if it had all been for naught. Hearing this passage in Advent causes us to ask where we have placed our hope and if we have allowed our hope to be dashed by difficult circumstances. Since Advent is as much about preparing for the Second Coming and Final Judgment as it is about preparing for the Nativity, the Baptist's situation offers a ripe opportunity for each of us to measure our own faith, trust, and hope in difficulty and darkness.

One of the best pieces of art to capture this moment is *St. John the Baptist in Prison*, painted by Juan Fernández de Navarrete in the latter half of the 1560s, while he was the court painter for King Philip II of Spain. This painting presents relatively few details, which means that we are able to focus intently on what is there. Like St. John stripped of his garments, our minds may be stripped down to the bare essentials for gauging our standing before God.

In this image, St. John sits alone in a prison cell, illuminated only by a little bit of light entering through a small, barred window. Perhaps this is an appropriate depiction of our feelings at many points throughout life. At some point, each of us has felt alone and in darkness, imprisoned in some way, with what seems like only a little light. Still, Advent is meant to remind us that a greater Light is coming, even in the midst of so much darkness. The season also offers us the opportunity to remember that even a little light will pierce the darkest darkness. We can therefore spend the last weeks of Advent asking which areas of our lives need to be illuminated, even just a little bit.

As he sits in his cell, John gazes on two important items with a very pensive look on his face. Clearly within his line of sight are the staff he carried and a red garment, symbolic of his impending martyrdom. The staff has been broken into a much smaller piece, which signifies that John's prophetic message has been cut off. The red garment lies in a pile, perhaps signifying that John may be asking whether or not his ministry was "worth the sacrifice," if it was effective, if it fulfilled its original mission. Is he still willing to suffer the fate that he seemed so willing to receive just a short time ago? These certainly might be questions that we need to ponder during Advent. Have my best-laid plans been thwarted? Have I been willing to speak prophetically when it was necessary and called for? Have I remained faithful, have I persevered in hope, despite the obstacles that have been before me? Where do I stand now?

Next we notice the position of John's body. The Baptist leans on a piece of wood. Some commentators might call it a table, but it resembles a gibbet on which criminals would have been crucified. This, of course, points the viewer specifically to the Cross of Jesus Christ. In every season of the life of discipleship, Advent included, each of us must realize that the fullness of the Christian life means embracing the Cross. It means leaning on Jesus, the Crucified Lord, as our only source of strength and hope. While John may not have heard this specifically, he lived, ministered, and died according to that paradigm. Will each of us embrace the Cross as John did?

One final detail in the painting is of great interest. There is a rope wrapped around John's right arm, near his wrist. Probably, this detail is meant to identify that the Baptist was bound and brought to this prison cell. Yet it is also symbolic for viewers in every age. After the Resurrection, Jesus promised St. Peter, "you will stretch out your hands, and another will dress you and carry you where you do not want to go" (John 21:18, ESV). Disciples of Jesus should realize that Jesus' statement is directed at each of us, individually. Advent is a time for every disciple to come to grips with this basic fact of the Christian life. We will be bound and led somewhere that we may not want to go. It might be a red martyrdom of death or a white martyrdom of purity and chastity, or it might mean becoming a social pariah for the sake of the truth of Jesus Christ.

This Gospel passage and this piece of art both serve to help us reflect on ways that we have been frustrated, and how we may feel that our hopes have been dashed. Additionally, they both inspire us to spend the remainder of the Advent season reflecting on the ways that God keeps our hope alive. It is inspiring to know that we can become a little bit like the greatest man born of woman, that we can heroically face disappointment and sorrow, and that we can prepare the way for Jesus. Our hope is renewed by these realizations and by engaging in the work that Our Blessed Lord asks of His disciples and prophets. Let's give thanks that God continues to sustain our hope during this season and always.

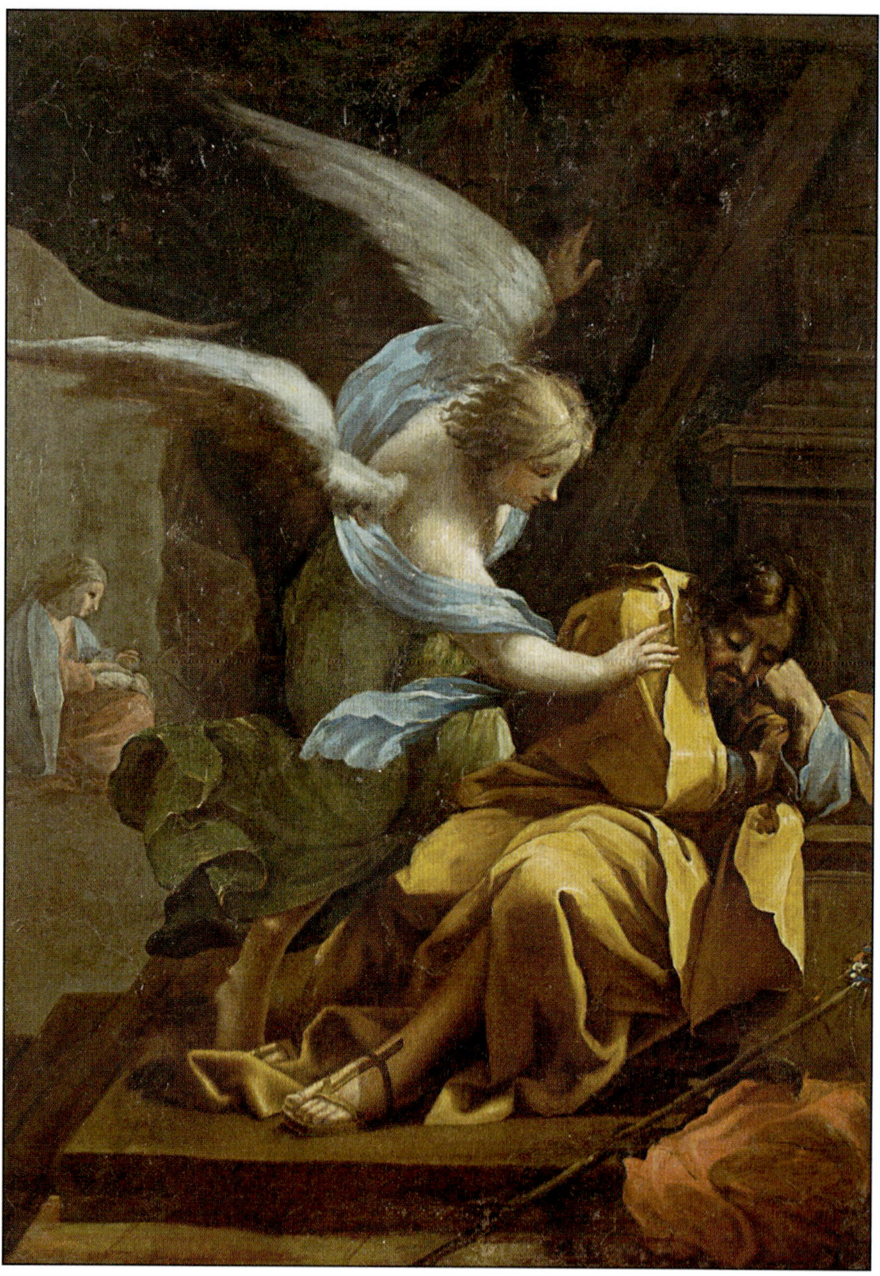

4

St. Joseph's Dream

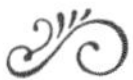

THE GOSPEL READINGS for the Fourth Sunday of Advent all tell of "how the birth of Jesus came about" (Matt. 1:18; see Matt 1:18–24; Luke 1:26–38, 39–45).[4] In the reading for Year A of the Church's liturgical calendar, we hear of Mary's mysterious and divine pregnancy. Then, we hear about the decision Joseph made to divorce Mary quietly, because "he was a righteous man." Next, we hear about the appearance of an angel in Joseph's dream, telling the young husband to "take Mary your wife into your home." After the description of the dream, we receive the author's commentary that this whole episode was the fulfillment of Isaiah's prophecy about Emmanuel, "God is with us." Finally, we hear of Joseph's decision after he awoke, to take "his wife into his home" (Matt. 1:18–24).

St. Joseph's Dream (*El Sueño de San José*) is one of Francisco Goya's earliest paintings, from the early 1770s. Like the biblical

[4] Art reflecting the themes of the readings for Years B and C of the Church's calendar will be discussed in the next two chapters.

passage, the painting is simple and understated. Yet, at the same time, it is clear and powerful. Right away, this painting draws viewers into the dramatic scene in Nazareth. In both cases, the Gospel scene and the painting, the few necessary details offer viewers ample opportunity for meditation during the final week of Advent as we prepare ourselves for the Nativity of Our Blessed Lord.

At the left-hand edge of the painting is a pregnant Mary. In this scene, Mary looks downcast and worried. One can imagine how anxious this teenage girl must have felt at this point in the story. Sure, she had ultimate trust in the Lord, but she might have worried that she would be divorced and ostracized in her small Jewish village. In these last days of Advent, we can ask the Lord to rescue us from our anxiety. We can ask Him to grant us the grace to grow in trust and learn to have faith that He will provide what we need with exactly the right timing.

At the opposite edge of the painting, we see the sleeping Joseph. One of the first things we note is St. Joseph's age and physical condition. In Goya's rendition of this scene, Joseph is young (no more than middle-aged) and virile. This coincides with a movement in recent generations to depict Joseph as a man who would walk to Bethlehem and Egypt and back, and who could be a strong protector and provider for the Holy Family of Nazareth. We can imagine that Joseph, in this moment, was exhausted not only from work but also from agonizing over his difficult decision. Advent offers each of us an opportunity to make two requests of the Lord, regardless of age. We can ask the Lord to help us surrender and rest as we make difficult decisions; and we can ask the Lord to fill us with the courage of St. Joseph, which was the courage to act on the message of the Lord.

Beside Joseph as he sleeps are a walking stick and some kind of red garment, both meant to signify Joseph's future in his relationship to Jesus and Mary. He would be told to walk from Nazareth to Bethlehem for a census with his wife who was near to delivering Jesus. Soon after that trek, Joseph would be told in another dream to take Jesus and Mary to Egypt for safety, an even more arduous pilgrimage. For both of these journeys, Joseph would need courage: courage to face the dangers of the road, and courage to accept the social ramifications of his decision. That is the courage of martyrdom. Each of us, regardless of age or life condition, needs to ask for such courage.

In the center of the painting is the messenger of the Lord. This angel's wings seem to bring us directly into Joseph's dreamy sleep. The angel's left hand reaches up to Heaven, while the right hand rests on Joseph's shoulder, signifying that the dream was a message conveyed directly from God to this man. During Advent, and as I ponder this piece of art, I ought to ask the Lord if there is any particular message that the Lord desires me to receive. I ought to ask the Lord to overcome my lack of awareness, even by the miraculous means of coming in a dream, if it is necessary.

We also can learn something important from Goya's use of color. Joseph is covered by a beige or brown tunic. Only his sleeves bear a little bit of vibrant color. This might be intended to convey his humanity and the fact that he was "a righteous man." His original decision was based on human righteousness, but his deep connection to God offered a glimmer of hope. Mary wears a magenta garment and a blue shawl. This might be the artist's attempt to convey that Mary was fully human but that she was cloaked in divine grace by means of the Immaculate Conception. Finally, the angel is wrapped in a garment of blue and green hues. The viewer quickly notices the contrast between the angel and Joseph, while Mary bears qualities of both. This observation provides an opportunity for the faithful to ask for the grace to be transformed and become more attuned to the Divine Voice and divine ways, and to ask for Our Lady's intercession in this process.

In this biblical narrative, the most hopeful part of the message is that Emmanuel, God with us, "will save his people from their sins" (Matt. 1:21). This line offers hope and consolation because it helps us to remember that we don't have to be the savior for ourselves or anyone else. Goya paints this reality well. Mary and Joseph are not active in this scene. They passively receive what God has to say and give. Thank goodness, during Advent, we can throw up our hands and admit that we don't have all the answers or the ability to solve every problem. We can become passive receivers of His divine grace, His message, while He ministers to all our needs.

Come, Lord Jesus, be with us in our needs and our weaknesses!

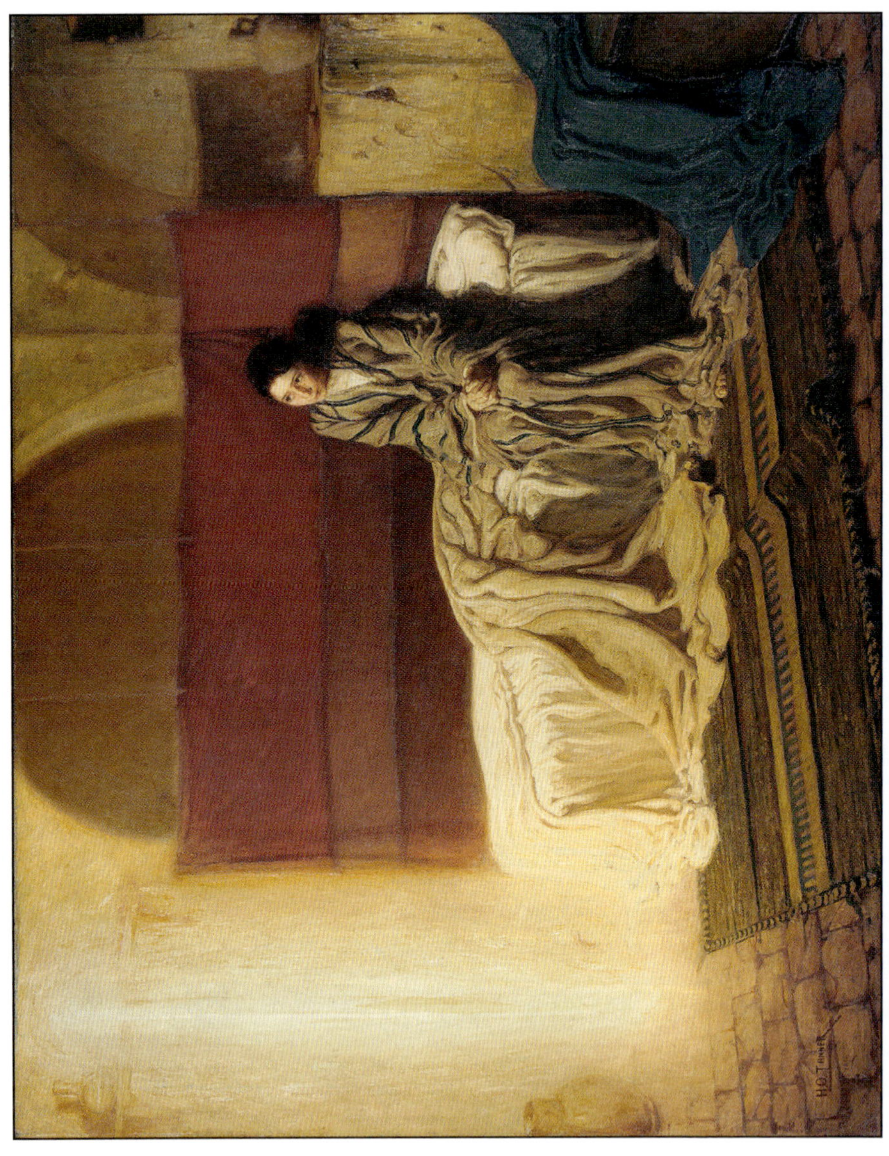

5

The Annunciation

IN YEAR B of the Church's liturgical calendar, the Gospel reading for the Fourth Sunday of Advent provides us with more details concerning God's preparation for the birth of Our Blessed Savior, specifically the Annunciation, the moment when Mary was presented with her call to bear the Son of God to the world (Luke 1:26–38). Mary's *fiat*, her "yes" to God's plan, opens the way to the Nativity at Bethlehem.

This moment has been depicted often and very beautifully in sacred art throughout Christian history. Think of Fra Angelico's *Annunciation*, for example. One of the finest of those depictions is by the American artist Henry Ossawa Tanner. His rendition of *The Annunciation* was painted in Paris in 1898, and its use of light and color has captivated Christian disciples ever since. This piece of art uses intricate details to tell the story and provides a fantastic opportunity for us to meditate on the reality of Advent and hope fulfilled in Jesus.[5]

[5] *The Annunciation*, by Henry Ossawa Tanner, is on display at the Philadelphia Museum of Art.

Tanner brings viewers to the authentic setting of a home in the ancient Near East. Small details such as a ruffled rug and an earthen jar add ambiance. The teenage girl, who is the focal point of the painting, sits on an unmade bed in a room that is partitioned from the rest of the house. As we meditate on this painting, these details can be indicative of our own minds, hearts, and lives, especially during Advent. Perhaps our proverbial houses for Jesus, our souls, are untidy or even unclean. This is why we need to access the Sacrament of Reconciliation during Advent. We need to make a suitable dwelling place for Jesus by tidying the messy areas of our souls.

In the center of the painting, we see Mary of Nazareth. Her folded hands indicate that she has been and continues to be in prayer. The look on her face gives the indication that we are privy to the moments while Mary is in dialogue with the angel, before her assent to the divine will. In the biblical narrative, listeners are informed that Mary was "greatly troubled" at Gabriel's greeting, "Hail, full of grace" (see Luke 1:28–29). This image seems to capture the moments while Mary "pondered what sort of greeting this might be." Advent makes a great time for each of us to reflect on how God wants to greet us and bring us many graces and blessings. Sure, none of us is "full of grace" like Mary, but God does want to bring each of us closer to Himself. Does that reality perplex and trouble me? Can I empathize with Mary's uncertainty about God's plan? Can I bring this confusion to God and have a prayerful conversation about it?

After we take in these details, we notice the object of Mary's gaze, the column of fiery light in another corner of her room. In his description of the Annunciation, Ven. Fulton Sheen called Gabriel the "Angel of Light [who] came down from the great Throne of Light."[6] Here, Tanner has captured Sheen's description and provided us with one of the best depictions of an angelic being in all of sacred art. Light, of course, is an appropriate theme during Advent. Light from the candles on Advent wreaths pierces the deepening darkness of winter. We anticipate that the Light of the World is coming into the world. Each of us might find it beneficial to spend a moment reflecting on how God's light has come into our lives, and how He might want to bring more light to us and through us.

Recognizing these details allows us to be drawn deeper into the remainder of the conversation. Gabriel speaks: "Do not be afraid, Mary," and "Behold, you will conceive in your womb and bear a son" (Luke 1:30–31). These two statements are intimately connected to God's movement throughout salvation history. Every time that God asks His people to take on a challenging task or mission, something that will bring abundant grace, He tells them not to fear. Throughout salvation history, sons have also held an important place: Isaac, Jacob, Joseph, and Solomon all point to the Incarnate Son of God who will reign on the throne of the everlasting Kingdom. Advent is a time to examine our personal history and to ask how God will help us overcome the fear that keeps us from living out His plan for our lives.

[6] Fulton J. Sheen, *Life of Christ* (New York: Image Books, 2008), 8.

In her exchange with Gabriel, Mary queries, "How can this be?" (Luke 1:34). Mary trusts God's message, but she wants to know how it will come about. Gabriel tells her first that "the power of the Most High will overshadow you," and then he announces to her Elisabeth's miraculous pregnancy (Luke 1:35–37). It is not inappropriate to ask God for verification about what He wants from us or what He wants to do in us. Advent is a great time to sit in the same posture as Mary, asking for clarity or verification about God's plan for our lives.

The biblical story tells about the final outcome. After this intense moment of prayer in which the recipient of God's message was confused, perplexed, and overwhelmed, Mary gives her consent, her *fiat*. She refers to herself as the "handmaid of the Lord" (Luke 1:38), which is a position of humility and assistance. During Advent, each of us can echo Mary's *fiat* by giving our consent for God to work in us by unusual and miraculous means; work that aids in His plan; work that will bring us to the fullness of who we are meant to be.

This piece of art provides at least part of a magnificent visual culmination of the Advent season. Coupled with the biblical narrative, this painting brings to life several of the most important themes of our spiritual lives, themes that we need to recognize and cultivate during Advent and every other season. Here's hoping that each of us makes our own respective *fiat* during this holy season, and that we allow the Incarnate God to be formed in us for the sake of the world.

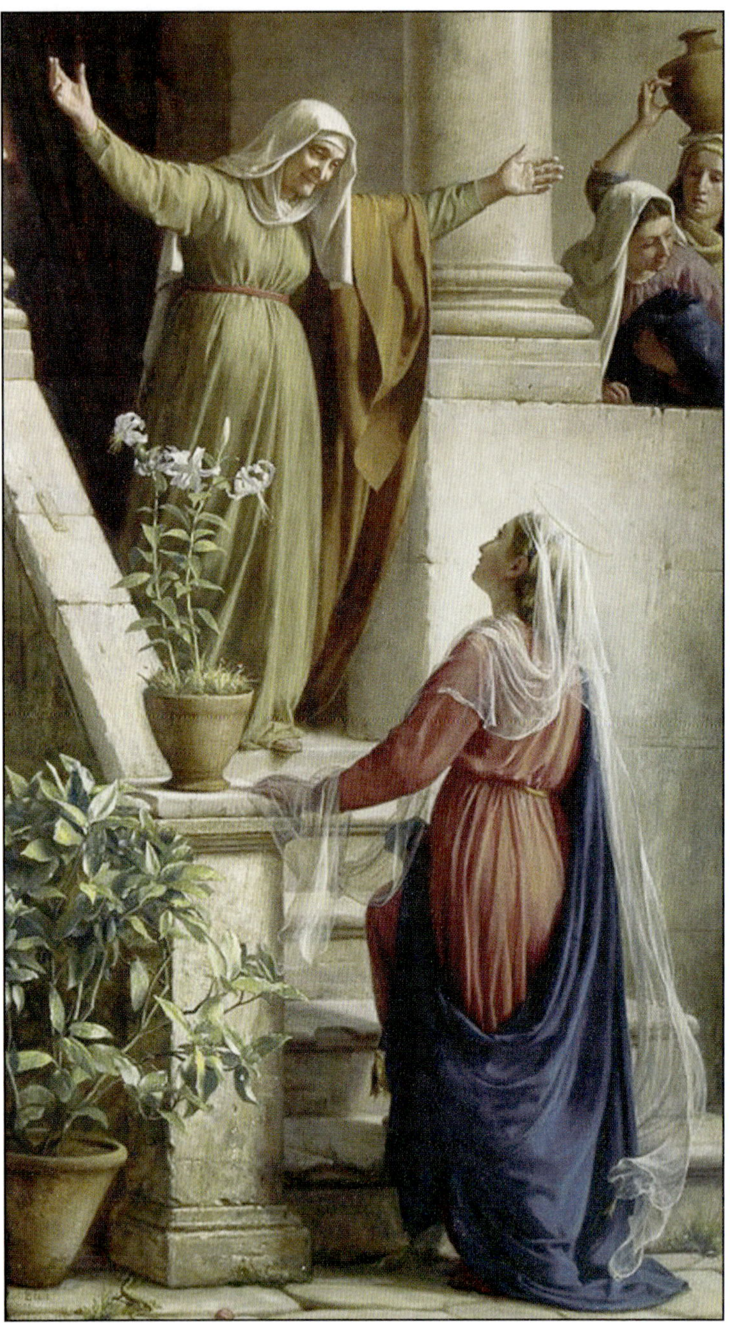

6

The Meeting of Mary and Elisabeth

The Gospel reading for the Fourth Sunday of Advent, Year C of the Church's liturgical calendar, tells us what happened after Mary made her *fiat* at the Annunciation. We hear that she "set out . . . in haste" from Nazareth. Her destination was the hill country of Judea, near Jerusalem, specifically the home of her kinswoman Elisabeth. At the Annunciation, the archangel Gabriel confirmed that he was God's messenger by informing Mary of her elder cousin's miraculous pregnancy. In this Gospel passage, we hear of the excitement between these two women. Elisabeth exclaims that Mary is "Most blessed . . . among women," and that the fruit of her womb is blessed. Finally, Elisabeth proclaims to Mary, "Blessed are you who believed that what was spoken to you by the Lord would be fulfilled" (Luke 1:39–45). This is a joyful encounter, a moment when both women know that God has finally answered their prayers and fulfilled His plan.

In 1866, Carl Heinrich Bloch painted *The Meeting of Mary and Elisabeth*.[7] Bloch's rendition of this biblical event is simple, but it captures Elisabeth's excitement and Mary's awe at what the Lord has done. This is a wonderful piece of art that gives us deeper insights into the Advent season and provides an appropriate final stop during our pilgrimage to the Nativity.

In the foreground of the painting, Mary stands at the bottom of the steps of Zechariah and Elisabeth's home. She wears the same blue garment that distinguishes her in so many pieces of sacred art. Still, more interesting than the blue mantle is the sheer veil that flows around her whole body. Bloch probably used this symbolic detail to highlight Mary's role as the Ark of the New Covenant. The veil is intended to shield this New Holy of Holies from the view of just any person. In this scene, only Elisabeth can see through the proverbial veil. During Advent, each of us can look to the Blessed Mother as the one who bears God to us. Specifically, we can ask her to pull back the veil that is over our eyes so that we can meet the Lord more fully.

While she stands at the bottom step, Mary gazes up at Elisabeth with a look that seems to express amazement at what has happened in both their lives. Even though she was sinless, Mary still would not have had the fullest understanding of God's exact plans. She would have needed that understanding to come in stages, sometimes through miracles. At this moment, she is in awe of the way God has worked to fulfill His plan. This can be our disposition during Advent too. We

7 *The Meeting of Mary and Elisabeth*, by Carl Bloch, is on display at the Brigham Young University Museum of Art in Provo, Utah.

recognize that we don't fully comprehend God's plan and His ways. We wait for fulfillment, and we stand in wonder as we recognize His miraculous movements.

It seems that Elisabeth, at the top of the steps, is the focal point of this painting. She bears a joyful look on her elderly face, and she stretches her arms wide to greet Mary. This is the moment when she "cried out in a loud voice and said, 'Most blessed are you among women' " (Luke 1:42). In her own joy and amazement, Elisabeth queries, "And how does this happen to me, that the mother of my Lord should come to me?" (Luke 1:43). During this blessed season, we want to capture St. Elisabeth's wonder and awe. Even though I am unworthy, I am happy and blessed that Mary sees fit to bring Jesus to me in a similar way that she brought Him to Elisabeth.

Bloch's rendition also draws a bit of attention to Elisabeth's pregnancy. Immediately, we think of the infant in her womb, John the Baptist, who "leaped for joy" at Mary's greeting (Luke 1:44). At this moment, our thoughts move forward in time to the Baptist's mission of pointing to the Messiah. In Advent, we need to mirror John's joy and zeal because Our Blessed Lord is nigh, and He is going to win salvation for us! Nearly everyone in this scene, even the one we cannot see, is wrapped in joy!

There are two other women, however, on the porch of the house who are not expressing the same joy. These women seem distracted by chores or other people out of the scene. While we don't know exactly what occupies these women, we can recognize that there are many things that can take our attention off of God's plan and His work. During Advent, we can prayerfully ask the Lord to help us focus in the midst of potential distractions and find true joy.

Between Mary and Elisabeth, in the visual center of the painting, stands a pot with flowers that seem to be lilies. Lilies, of course, represent rebirth, purity, virtue, and innocence. These two women provide us with a deeper appreciation for each of these qualities. They are especially models of fidelity, even in the midst of uncertainty. This detail ought to remind us that Advent is a blessed time in which each of us can ask for a renaissance by the Lord's grace, a rebirth facilitated by growing in virtues of faith and purity.

Bloch's painting of this biblical event makes a fitting culmination of our Advent pilgrimage with art. We have seen how Advent prepares us to avoid falling into the patterns of "the days of Noah." We have heard the call to repentance made by the Voice Crying Out in the Desert. We have empathized with John in his despair at not seeing the completion of God's plan. Finally, we can enter into the joy and wonder of these women at the ways God unexpectedly, miraculously fulfills His plan. These final dispositions are ultimately what God wants us to have during Advent and all year long. May we all experience such joy and wonder in the last days of Advent, during the Christmas season, and beyond.

PART II

The Art of Christmas & Jesus' Childhood

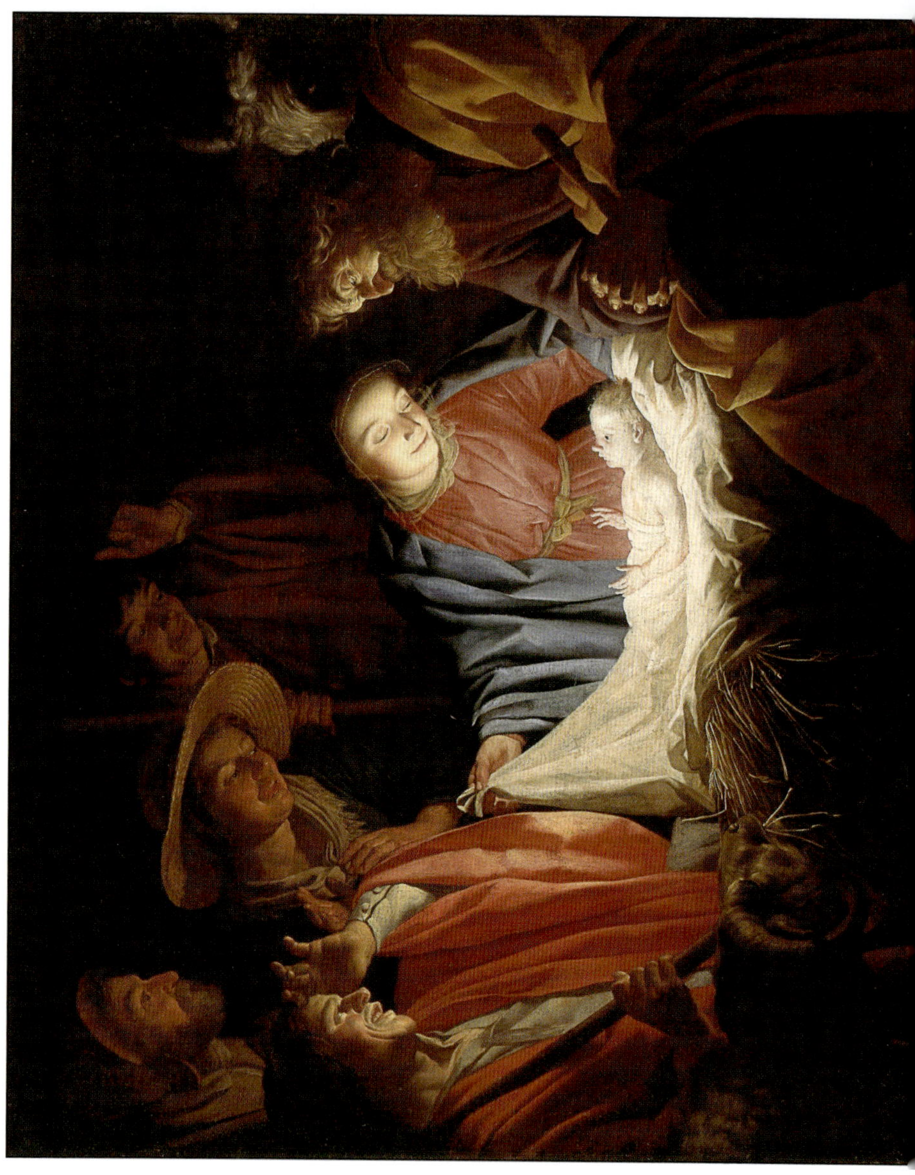

I

Adoration of the Shepherds

THERE ARE MANY beautiful depictions in sacred art of the Nativity of Our Lord. Among these, *Adoration of the Shepherds* by Gerard van Honthorst, from the early seventeenth century, is surely one of the most recognizable. This work offers a visual depiction of the Christmas event that draws the viewer quickly into the scene and, more importantly, allows the viewer to grasp the depths of the mystery of the Incarnation that it portrays.

The very first detail a viewer notices upon approaching this work is the stark contrast between the dark perimeter and the light at the very center. Such contrast was a device commonly employed by the Utrecht Caravaggisti, a group of Dutch painters among whom Honthorst worked and who were influenced deeply by Caravaggio, the Italian master of *chiaroscuro*, the technique of creating a deep contrast between darkness and light. Honthorst's *Adoration of the Shepherds* is among the most memorable examples of this captivating technique. Before viewers ever begin to examine the finer details of the painting, his use of *chiaroscuro* immediately opens up the opportunity for reflection on the interplay, even the tension, of spiritual illumination and darkness in all of our lives.

At the center of the painting is the source of illumination, the Infant Jesus. This focus makes the evangelical and catechetical point that Jesus, the Incarnate Emmanuel, is the light at the center of a world shrouded in darkness. He radiates light and truth and love outward. And so the painting sends an obvious invitation to the viewer: Come out of the darkness and toward the light. What needs to happen for me to be ready, willing, or able to begin that journey toward fuller light?

Just above the newborn Messiah is His Mother, Mary. She wears red, which in art is often symbolic of humanity, but she is cloaked in a mantle of blue, which is symbolic of the divine realm. We know that Mary is human, which should make her relatable to each of us; but she is also immaculately conceived and "full of grace," which allows her to reflect the light from Jesus to the rest of the dark world more fully. Finally, we notice that Mary wears a look of deep peace and contentment on her face, as though her vocation has culminated in this moment.

These details invite the viewer to ponder a range of questions about Jesus, Mary, and the life of discipleship. How do I relate to the Blessed Mother? How has she allowed me to bask in the light of her Divine Son? How can I find a similar peace and contentment for my own life? How can I reflect the Light of Christ and His glory to others around me?

Beside the manger, at the right side of the painting, we see St. Joseph. He appears aged, symbolizing wisdom and righteousness as described by the evangelist (see Matt. 1:19). He gazes at the newborn Lord with his hands folded in prayer, the source of his righteousness. In his lap, he holds a walking staff, significant of the many long walks he would undertake with this Holy Family, to Egypt and then back-and-forth to festival celebrations in Jerusalem. Still, it is the look on his face that captures the viewer's attention most. Recalling the few details we know about St. Joseph from the biblical record, we might surmise that he is caught up in a moment of reflecting on the dream in which he was told to name this Messiah Emmanuel. Have I sought wisdom by gazing upon the Incarnate Word of God? Do I reflect, from time to time, on the private revelations that God has provided to inspire my walk of discipleship? Am I ready and willing to take up a challenging journey or task that might be asked of me?

On the other side of the manger, and behind Mary, are the shepherds who have come to Bethlehem from the surrounding fields. The shepherd closest to the viewer seems to shield his eyes from the light emitted by the Incarnate Word of God. Two other shepherds raise their arms, making gestures of praise, as if to echo the angelic chorus they had heard in the field before coming into the city. The fourth shepherd wears a look of amazed astonishment. "Is this real?" he seems to ask. "Can I be witnessing this miracle unfold?" Have I had dispositions like these in my own spiritual life?

In the shadows of the painting, at the bottom-left and top-right corners, respectively, are a ram and an ox. The artist may have intended to evoke the presence of these animals in the worship of the Old Covenants. Of course, there is the memorable scene, recorded in Genesis 22, in which Abraham took his son, Isaac, up Mount Moriah to sacrifice him at God's command, and at the last moment, his son was spared and a ram was provided as a sacrifice in his stead. And in the prescriptions for worship given to the Israelites while they wandered in the desert, both animals are prescribed as specific parts of the atonement sacrifice (see Lev. 8–9, for example). But throughout the Old Testament is the constant refrain that there is a better, purer sacrifice that the Lord intends than simply burnt animal offerings. In Samuel's preaching to King Saul, for example, he proclaimed, "Obedience is better than sacrifice, to listen, better than the fat of ram" (1 Sam. 15:22). And later, King David, who was anointed by Samuel, prayed with this truth as he wrote the psalms: "I may praise God's name in song and glorify it with thanksgiving. That will please the Lord more than oxen, more than bulls with horns and hooves" (Ps. 69:31–32).

The artist quite probably employed both of these animals to point to the Perfect Sacrifice at the center of the scene. He gives visual expression to the same truth that was taught by the author of the Letter to the Hebrews: "For it is impossible that the blood of bulls and goats take away sins." Instead, the author reminds us, "we have been consecrated through the offering of the body of Jesus Christ once for all" (Heb. 10:4, 10).

Jesus, Emmanuel, will save His people from their sins specifically by providing a perfect sacrifice of atonement, something rams and bulls could never do. Do I see Jesus through this lens, realizing that His whole mission was to atone for, to set right, what human sin had thrown askew?

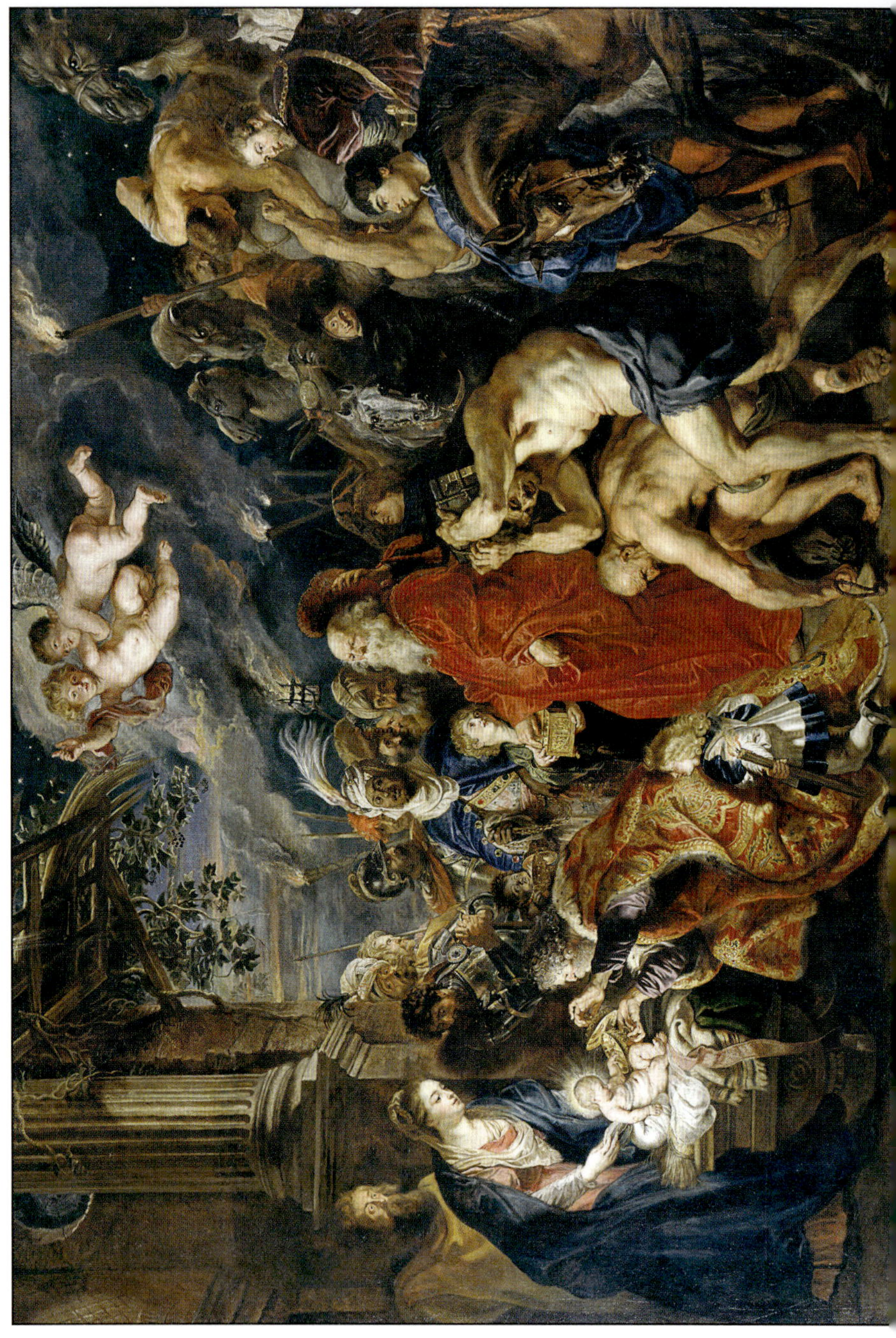

2

Adoration of the Magi

THROUGHOUT CHRISTIAN HISTORY, the Feast of the Epiphany has perpetually been one of the most cherished celebrations of the mystery of salvation. This biblical event is the first manifestation of Jesus to the world beyond the geographic and cultural boundaries of ancient Israel. As such, it beckons us to meditate on Jesus as *Lumen Gentium*, Light to the Nations.

There have been quite a few significant renditions of this event throughout the ages, each having great merit. Yet Peter Paul Rubens's *Adoration of the Magi*, completed in 1629, stands above the others. Rubens's masterpiece is worthy of our attention because it leads us so deeply into meditation on the historical and spiritual reality of this moment in the life and mission of Jesus.[8]

The first thing that a viewer of this painting notices is the vibrant display of color, a trend very common in Rubens's work

[8] The painting that was finished in 1629, which now hangs in the Museo del Prado in Madrid, Spain, is a remastered version. The artist also painted this scene in at least three previous versions, and one later version.

throughout his career. Reds and blues and golds dominate the scene; these colors signify God's glory and the celebration taking place at the meeting of humanity with divinity. There are also prominent accents of purple and green, which signify new life and the regeneration of the soul. Lastly, there are also half a dozen flames accenting the event. While these flames have a specific purpose in the historical depiction of the event, their colors also point viewers back to the light and warmth of God's love.

The nascent Lord is the focal point of the painting, made prominent by bright white swaddling clothes and a gold halo around His head. The Infant's tiny hand reaches out to touch the gold presented to Him by one of the Magi. All things point to His purity and royalty, both of which ultimately point to His divinity. Such details cause the viewer to ask: Am I ready to acclaim Jesus as the Lord and center of my life, even amid all the other exciting and beautiful details around me? Am I ready to bring Him whatever beautiful and precious gifts I can muster?

Just in front of Jesus and behind the one kneeling Magi, at the center of the painting, are at least two other Magi, accompanied by a whole retinue of servants, horses, and dromedaries. The caravan is made up of figures of widely variant ages, nationalities, and even economic conditions. This diverse crowd is clearly the artist's depiction of the whole world outside of the covenant people, all coming to meet the Son of God. This image ought to bring the viewer to a deeper appreciation of the history of God's covenant relationship with Israel, which has been expanded to the whole world through Jesus Christ.

Do I have a deep appreciation for God's Chosen People, Israel? Do I see how the New Covenant is related to the Old, growing and benefitting from it?

At the left-hand edge of the painting, behind Jesus, Mary and Joseph appear. Mary holds up the Infant Lord while Joseph bears a look of astonishment on his face. His look seems to indicate that he is still bewildered at the ways God is fulfilling His prophetic messages. Do I seek to foster devotion to the Blessed Mother and St. Joseph, which will lead me more fully into relationship with Jesus? How do I emulate their attitudes and actions in my daily approach to discipleship?

Given the prominence of the Holy Family in this image, the viewer should notice and consider their position in relation to the Magi and their caravan. The Gospel tells us that the Magi followed a star "until it came and stopped over the place where the child was.... And on entering the house, they saw the child with Mary his mother. They prostrated themselves and did him homage" (Matt. 2:9, 11). While the biblical text indicates that they did not see the newborn Lord until after they entered the house, Rubens places the Messiah on the threshold as the Magi approach, seemingly while they "rejoiced exceedingly." The artist's depiction, while not completely faithful to the biblical text, is fruitful still. It shows the divine coming out to encounter mankind; it shows God's Chosen People, Israel, coming to meet the nations; and it shows that both sides have made an effort to arrive at this place of encounter. That is a significant theological, pastoral, and moral realization for all of us as we seek truth, goodness, and beauty during this earthly pilgrimage.

One of the Magi kneels in front of Jesus and presents a container of gold. Another Magi, cloaked in blue, holds a censer, which seems to burn with the incense they have brought as the second traditional gift. The third Magi, cloaked in red, reaches into a golden box, seemingly in preparation to present the myrrh (Matt. 2:11). This completes the triumvirate of gifts that acclaim Jesus' role as King of all nations, as the final Messenger of God's plan, as the eternal High Priest who offers the perfect sacrifice to the Heavenly Father.

Just to the left of this third Magi (to the viewer's right) are two slaves clad only in loincloths. They labor with large bags and boxes. Perhaps the artist intended to depict that far more gold, frankincense, and myrrh were presented than just individual jars. If these men were prominent cultural figures from the East, they probably had more than mere small containers of each of the gifts. Quite simply, the Magi would have given prodigiously. This detail, and the reality it illuminates, might cause the viewer to consider his or her own generous gifts to the Lord: How much of my precious gifts am I willing to present to God? Do I hold anything back?

Layered behind the crowd in the forefront are Roman soldiers with pikes and blazing torches. These soldiers point toward the slaughter of innocents commanded by King Herod out of his wicked envy. The dark, violent sky in the background also provides a portent to that tragedy. Yet the artist might also have used this detail to situate this event within an important historical context. The Messiah, the New King of Nations, had come to bring the good news of peace and salvation to the whole world, and he would do that through the empire that had subdued the world through the Pax Romana.

Finally, at the top of the scene are two cherub angels. One of them points upward, perhaps as if he is reminding the Magi of the prophetic star that had guided them to this location but is not depicted in this scene. The artist may also have meant for these messengers to signify the message given to the Magi in a dream that will warn them not to visit Herod on their return. By following that admonition, the Magi would have been executing the plan of the Father of All Nations rather than that of a relatively minor provincial political power.

With his rendition of this biblical event, Rubens has given viewers a wonderful opportunity to ponder several important tenets of God's impeccable providence. We are beckoned to consider His work through His covenant people, Israel, at the same time that we see how He brought all the other nations into that covenant relationship. We are able to ponder how the New Israel, the Church, consists of all types of persons of varying ages and life conditions. And in the very final analysis, we are brought to a precipice point of asking ourselves if we are willing, with the Magi, to fall down and worship Him, offering the very best gifts that we have.

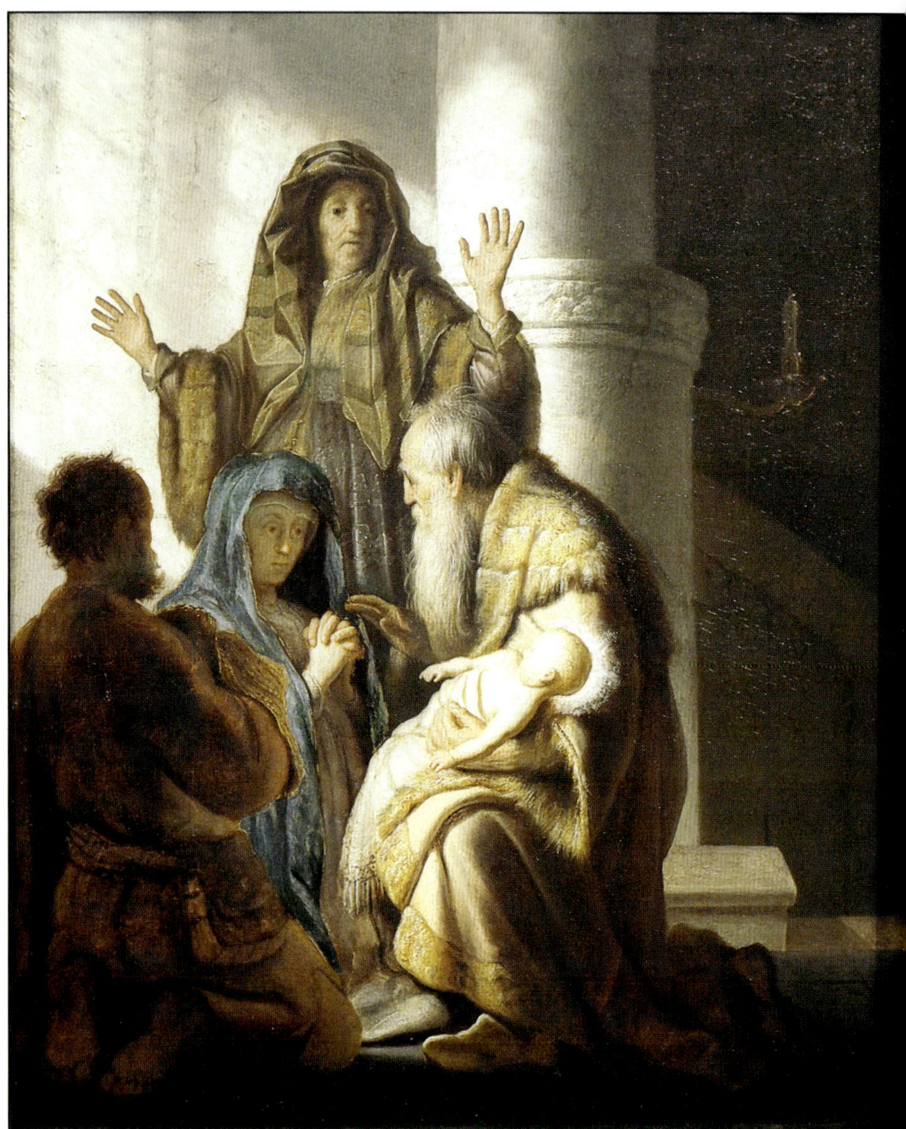

3

Simeon and Anna in the Temple

The Presentation of Jesus in the Temple marks the transition from celebrating the Christmas season to reflecting on Jesus' childhood, including the hidden years at Nazareth. This memorable biblical scene is only recorded in St. Luke's Gospel. The biblical record of this event is filled with allusions to memorable scenes and prophecies from the Old Testament, such as the birth and dedication of Samuel and hopeful words spoken to the fickle nation of Israel by Isaiah. It is also the source of one of the three great Gospel canticles prayed by Christian posterity, the Canticle of Simeon, also known as the *Nunc Dimittis*. All these details ripen this episode for viewers as we ponder the mystery of salvation through sacred art.

From the Middle Ages into modernity, artists have rendered this event on canvas. One of the most insightful depictions was produced by Rembrandt van Rijn in 1627, *Simeon and Anna in the Temple*. The choices that the artist made in light, color, position, and facial expression of characters all lead the viewer into a deeper understanding of one of the Dutch master's great works and into fruitful prayer and reflection about the spiritual life.

From the earliest moments of gazing on Rembrandt's painting, the viewer notices a stark contrast between light and dark. Some areas of the Temple remain darkened, but the light that floods the scene from the top left draws the viewer's eyes directly to Jesus, the ultimate source of spiritual illumination, the One who would declare himself the New Temple (see John 2:19–21). This detail causes us to remember the final phrases of Simeon's canticle, "a light for revelation to the Gentiles, and for glory to your people Israel" (Luke 2:32). Light in the painting might also cause the viewer to hear the prophetic words of Isaiah: "Then the glory of the Lord shall be revealed" (Isa. 40:5); and "I formed you, and set you as a covenant for the people, a light for the nations, to open the eyes of the blind, to bring out . . . from the dungeon those who live in darkness" (Isa. 42:6–7). The evangelist and the artist both seek to depict Jesus as the Light from God filling the Temple after years, even centuries, of darkness.

This detail, and our reflection on these biblical passages, might cause us to ask: Has there been darkness in my life, recently or even for some long period of time? Have I been waiting in despondency, or have I allowed God's promises to be a source of hope? Have I been able to find restored, greater hope in Jesus, specifically in His Real Presence in the Eucharist?

Rembrandt paints the Infant Messiah in Simeon's arms. Presumably, the old man who had been "awaiting the consolation of Israel" (Luke 2:25) has already proclaimed his canticle, "Master, you may let your servant go in peace" (Luke 2:29).

We glean this because he leans in to speak to Mary, and her eyes are wide with astonishment. Surely, she would have been ready to hear about her divine Son as the source of Israel's redemption; but she would have been shocked to hear the portion of the prophecy spoken directly to her: "Behold, this child is destined for the fall and rise of many in Israel, and to be a sign that will be contradicted (and you yourself a sword will pierce), so that the thoughts of many hearts may be revealed" (Luke 2:34–35).

Simeon's prophecy also opens up to us a devotion to Our Lady of Sorrows. First revealed to St. Bridget of Sweden in the fourteenth century, this devotion brings a person closer to Jesus by meditating on the seven moments of sorrow and agony experienced by Mary of Nazareth as recorded in the Gospels. In the modern era, Ven. Fulton Sheen also meditated on this biblical episode and its corresponding devotion. In his book *Life of Christ*, the great teacher helped his readers understand that identification with Jesus' suffering was essential to Mary's exalted role.[9] One comes to view Our Lady's sorrows as seven swords thrust into her heart—paths by which she was united to the Passion of her Son, Jesus, and by which each of us can connect more deeply with both Mary and Jesus. It would be difficult to find anyone who has not experienced at least some level of suffering in life. All of us, then, ought to find some compassion and solace from Our Blessed Mother, who knows suffering as well as anyone.

Behind Simeon and Mary stands Anna, the prophetess who "never left the temple, but worshipped night and day

[9] Sheen, *Life of Christ*, 32–38.

with fasting and prayer" (Luke 2:37). Rembrandt captures an important detail, as he depicts Anna raising her hands in surprise, praise, and gratitude. It is easy to imagine her response to this moment, as we read in St. Luke's account that she "spoke about the child to all who were awaiting the redemption of Jerusalem" (Luke 2:38). This reveals a pattern in the life of discipleship: first we give thanks and praise for the fulfillment of God's plan, and then we are called to go tell others. Reflecting on this part of the scene, the viewer might ask: If I am seeking God's fulfilled plans, or even a miracle, do I, like Anna, take up a posture of constant prayer and worship? How do I react when God answers, even in an unexpected way? Am I quick to share with others the good news of God's fulfilled promises?

A viewer cannot turn away without pondering the last figure in the painted scene, St. Joseph. The way Jesus' earthly father is depicted offers a rich meditation on a few points. First is Joseph's orientation: he is turned away from the viewer. Many artists have used the technique of a character turned away from the viewer (and toward the focal point of the scene) to invite deeper meditation. Next, Joseph kneels. Recalling that none of Joseph's words are recorded in the Gospels, we might recognize that the posture of our bodies can speak as loudly as any words that pass through our lips. Kneeling is a sign of invoking God's providence, favor, and mercy. Finally, Joseph is positioned mostly in the penumbra of the Temple. This might lead us to ponder the fact that all fallen humans (including ourselves) lead lives marked at times by greater and less illumination. This realization might lead me to desire and seek more light. In each of these ways, we are invited to place ourselves in Joseph's position.

How do I approach this scene? Do I seek to exist in the light more than in the shadows? How do I understand and appropriate the actions and words of each character in the scene? If I think and act differently, especially when it comes to Jesus, will I exist more in the light where I desire to be?

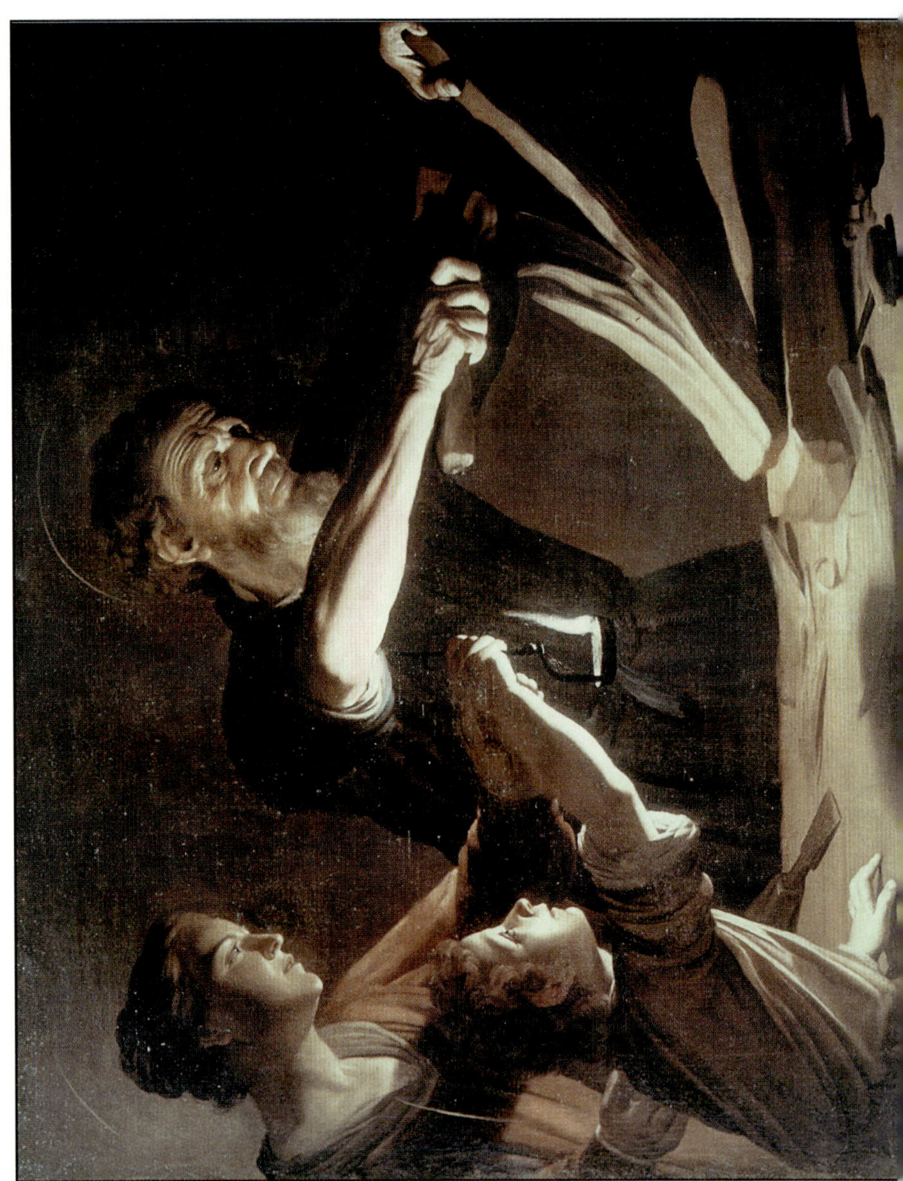

4

The Holy Family in the Carpenter Shop

THE MOST MYSTERIOUS part of Jesus' life, the part about which we know least, is the period of quiet years in Nazareth. We know nothing of the life of the Holy Family during and after their exile in Egypt, except what St. Luke tells us at the end of his account of the Presentation in the Temple: "The child grew and became strong, filled with wisdom; and the favor of God was upon him" (Luke 2:40). We know intuitively, though, that this period of years, especially Jesus' childhood, was formative and crucial for the choices and decisions He would make during His public ministry. Thus, it is both mysterious and fascinating to ponder what the young Messiah learned during those quiet years in Nazareth, and we must allow our imaginations to do a little bit of work.

Gerard van Honthorst aids our imaginations with his captivating piece, *The Holy Family in the Carpenter Shop*.[10] Completed in 1610, the painting employs the artist's signature

[10] *The Holy Family in the Carpenter Shop*, by Gerard van Honthorst, is on display at the Museum and Gallery at Bob Jones University in Greenville, South Carolina.

technique and detail. Honthorst aids the viewer in placing himself or herself in this intimate scene, which then facilitates an unfolding of imaginative ruminations about that quiet life by the Sea of Galilee. As if guided by the Holy Spirit, the viewer soon begins pondering how he or she would feel and develop in the same setting.

The very first detail apparent to the viewer is the artist's use of *chiaroscuro*, the deep contrast between darkness and light in the scene. This, of course, is apropos to the historical reality, since we know little about the life of the Holy Family in Nazareth. We simply know that the Incarnate Word was raised quietly by His Virgin Mother and her husband, who was a carpenter and "a righteous man" (Matt. 1:19). In a fascinating way, Honthorst uses the darkness at the edges of the scene as a shroud, something to protect a great mystery within. Hopefully, this causes the viewer to ask: Am I willing to enter behind that shroud, where I may come to learn deeper truths about God and myself?

Once the viewer has made that decision to enter in, the artist uses his signature detail of a single candle to provide the illumination for the scene. The viewer notices a young Jesus, maybe eight or ten years old, holding the candle and watching his earthly father's craft intently. This provides a visual depiction of Luke 2:40 (quoted above) and reminds us that part of Jesus' growth in Nazareth was in intellect and practical skill. No matter my age or life status, am I able and willing to acknowledge that I need to continue developing attitudes, knowledge, and skills that will bring me to my full stature as a human person?

Mary is behind Jesus, clad in red garments. The color might be representative of her humanity, from whence Jesus received His full human nature. It might also be representative of Mary's sacrifice, as she willingly gave over her Son to His mission of saving and redeeming mankind. As such, it might also have been the artist's particular way of pointing to the seven sorrows of Mary, which were prophesied by Simeon at Jesus' Presentation in the Temple.

Mary's right hand is on Jesus' shoulder, while her left hand guides His extended arm holding the candle. This posture reminds us again that Our Blessed Lord required guidance and assistance as He grew. It was Mary, specifically, who taught Him about the Spirit of God and about the Law that He was fulfilling. Does this reflection help me to recall those who have been tender and stabilizing influences in my own life? Who has guided me to know and love truth, goodness, and beauty? For whom else might I provide that stabilizing and formative influence? A spouse and children? Extended family? Students? Someone else in my community?

At the center of the painting, behind the candle, is Joseph. The viewer might immediately notice his age. While he does not seem elderly, he does seem to be at the twilight of middle age. This is probably the artist's way of giving visual expression to the saint's wisdom and virtue, both of which develop as a result of much significant life experience. This causes the viewer to ponder: Am I growing in wisdom and virtue? Do I learn, even the hard lessons, from my experiences? Do I recognize that life's pleasures and travails both are useful for bringing me to the fullness of who God intends me to be?

Whatever his age, Joseph works intently with a hand tool to form a piece of wood. It seems that the object he creates would be for use around their home. Other tools of his trade, along with pieces of shaved wood, lie around the table. What skills have I learned throughout my life that can be used to make and manage a home? At the same time, are there aspects of my life, even small ones, that must be shaved away and discarded so that something beautiful can be displayed?

Joseph's eyes look prayerfully focused, indicating that his work, his creative output, was a work of prayer throughout the process. Ours ought to be so too. Whether I am a painter, an engineer, a dentist, a custodian, or a vehicle mechanic, do I pray throughout my work? Do I make my work a part of my prayer to God? Do I make my work a sacrificial offering so some greater good can come about?

Finally, it is appropriate to meditate on the parents together as a single reality. It is clear that both Mary and Joseph contribute in essential, and essentially unique, ways to Jesus' human development. This ought to remind us of the necessity of a mother and father in the life of every human child. Neither can replace or supplant the qualities provided by the other. To become who He was, Jesus needed what both His parents offered to Him. How do I ensure that my children have what both a mother and father offer uniquely? Have I deprived something essential to someone entrusted to my care? Has someone deprived this essential thing to me? How can I rectify that? How can I flourish beyond that lack? Am I called to provide this essential thing to someone who might lack it otherwise? Do I let the wisdom of God guide me in answering these questions, or do I act from my fallen tendencies?

In *The Holy Family in the Carpenter Shop*, Gerard van Honthorst has provided the world with a masterpiece, both technically and spiritually. In addition to helping viewers learn about artistic style and mechanics, this painting has the potential to aid each of us in recognizing that we all have moments and periods of life in which we enter a proverbial Nazareth. Recognizing that fact, and entering prayerful meditation on our mundane, hidden lives, allows each of us to realize the opportunities present to us, even our muck and mess, that are shrouded in darkness to the rest of the world.

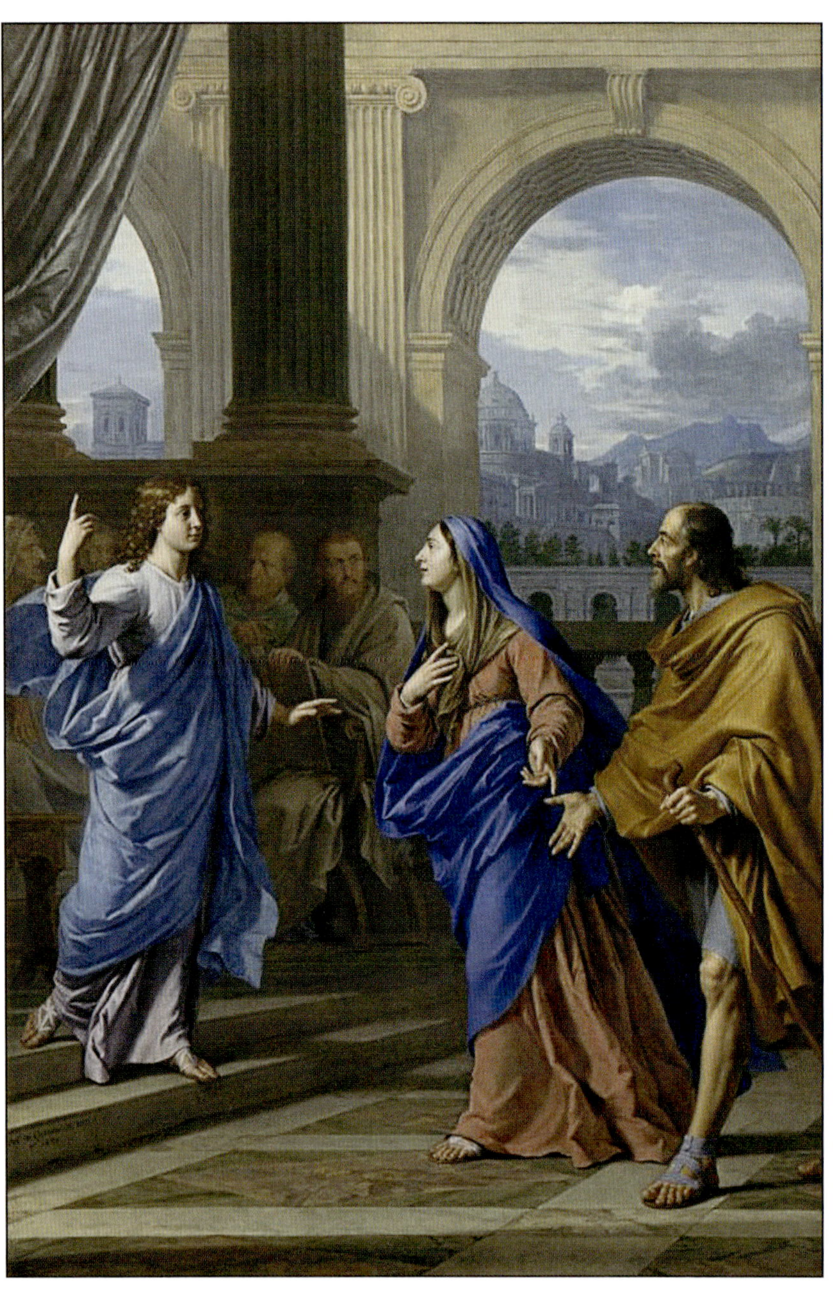

5

Christ among the Doctors

THE LAST RECORDED episode of Jesus' childhood in the Gospels is the Messiah being found in the Temple "when he was twelve years old" (Luke 2:42). This episode highlights the importance of the Passover in Jewish culture, the faithfulness of the Holy Family of Nazareth to the Mosaic Law, and the obedience habituated by the developing God-Man. Beyond those basic details, we also glean Jesus' awareness that He, in His own divine Personhood, is the fulfillment of Temple worship. It is a memorable moment that serves as a clear signpost of mysterious things to come.

Many artists have depicted this biblical event in varying eras and styles, from Duccio to Veronese to Tissot to Hunt. Among these, Philippe de Champaigne's rendition, *Christ among the Doctors*, finished in 1663, provides a visual complement to the biblical passage that opens a deep and rich moment of prayer for the viewer.

The painting is set inside a stone and marble structure, which is clearly supposed to be the Temple in Jerusalem. There are, however, large archways and porticos that allow the viewer to see beyond the immediate scene. By this method, Champaigne envelopes the scene in blue, the color of the heavenly realm. Even inside, there are distinct patches of blue, especially the cloaks worn by Jesus and Mary. These clearly indicate Jesus' own divinity and Mary's having been overshadowed by the Holy Spirit at the Annunciation and the Incarnation. This important detail of color might cause the viewer to ask: Do I see the heavenly realm, God's divinity, enveloping every aspect of my life, surrounding me and drawing me into itself?

In the background there are also patches of green. Even one of the depicted teachers wears the color. Given that green in art symbolizes hope and regeneration, we can understand that this points to the amazement these scholars had at Jesus' understanding (see Luke 2:47). Am I amazed and astonished by Jesus Christ? Am I able to hear His words, His teachings, His miracles as sources of hope and regeneration for my own life? Even if I have studied and understood deeply, is there some new and fascinating aspect of God's revelation that can amaze me, just as the scholars were amazed at Jesus?

Champaigne also invites the viewer to deeper reflection through his use of color on St. Joseph. Joseph is cloaked in a brownish-gold vestment. Perhaps the artist intentionally painted the cloak to convey multiple qualities, as brown would symbolize his humanity and gold would symbolize his virtuous character. Such a deft use of color causes the viewer to ponder his or her own connection with St. Joseph: How is it possible to overcome the stain of Original Sin by a righteous life? Do I recognize my fallen nature and sinful tendencies while I continue to strive for virtue and holiness? Despite my sinfulness, how am I called to serve as a righteous leader for my family or for other groups?

The hands of the two parents provide opportunities for fruitful meditation. Mary's left hand and Joseph's right hand are almost touching. Their posture indicates the query that they made to Jesus: "Son, why have you done this to us?" (Luke 2:48). Mary's right hand touches her chest, perhaps indicating that she has some vague understanding of the deeper revelation of His words and actions. More specifically, the artist here gives visual expression to the fact that she "kept all these things in her heart" (Luke 2:51).

A recognition of these minute details elicits deeper questions about personal psychology. Have I been exceedingly anxious because I have felt that I lost something important, even beyond material things? Perhaps I have been anxious about the way a certain relationship has been changing, or about a lack of order in my own life. In those moments, have I stopped to think and pray about how I could be about God's business instead of focused on my own anxiety?

Jesus' hands also illuminate deeper truths behind the words recorded on the Sacred Page. His left hand seems to be telling His parents to calm down a bit, but it is His right hand that emphasizes the point of the whole episode. Jesus points upward, as if to His heavenly Father. In the biblical text, Jesus responds to His parents' query with a question of His own: "Did you not know that I must be about my father's business?" (Luke 2:49, Douay-Rheims).

The story's conclusion indicates something important as well. After Jesus asks His question, there is no specific verbal response. We only learn that Mary and Joseph "did not understand." Yet Jesus responded to His own question with action. "He went down with them . . . and was obedient to them" (Luke 2:50–51). The young Messiah knew and exhibited His heavenly Father's business, which was to go and obediently engage in the business of Nazareth. That is how He grew most certainly in wisdom and favor while He was in Nazareth, preparing for His public ministry.

This single important detail opens up important considerations for our own moral lives. First, how do I respond to the call to obedience? Do I struggle to give due deference to those who have legitimate authority over me? Even if I submit, do I do so with grumbling and bitterness? Or do I find ways to submit with trust and joy?

A final consideration is the duration of the life of obedience at Nazareth. From this point, it was roughly eighteen more years before Jesus began His public ministry, and more than twenty until the full accomplishment of His mission. Am I content with extended periods of little or no "productive" movement? Can I be satisfied with being unknown, even forgotten, by the wider world? Without a doubt, in these details, Jesus has provided each of us with a profound example, dynamic traits by which to grow in age, wisdom, and grace.

While it is relatively simple, Champaigne's work of art especially helps us to ponder this final point. It is that simple, quiet, and trusting obedience that will help us attain the heavenly realm to which Jesus points in the painting.

PART III

The Art of Lent & Holy Week

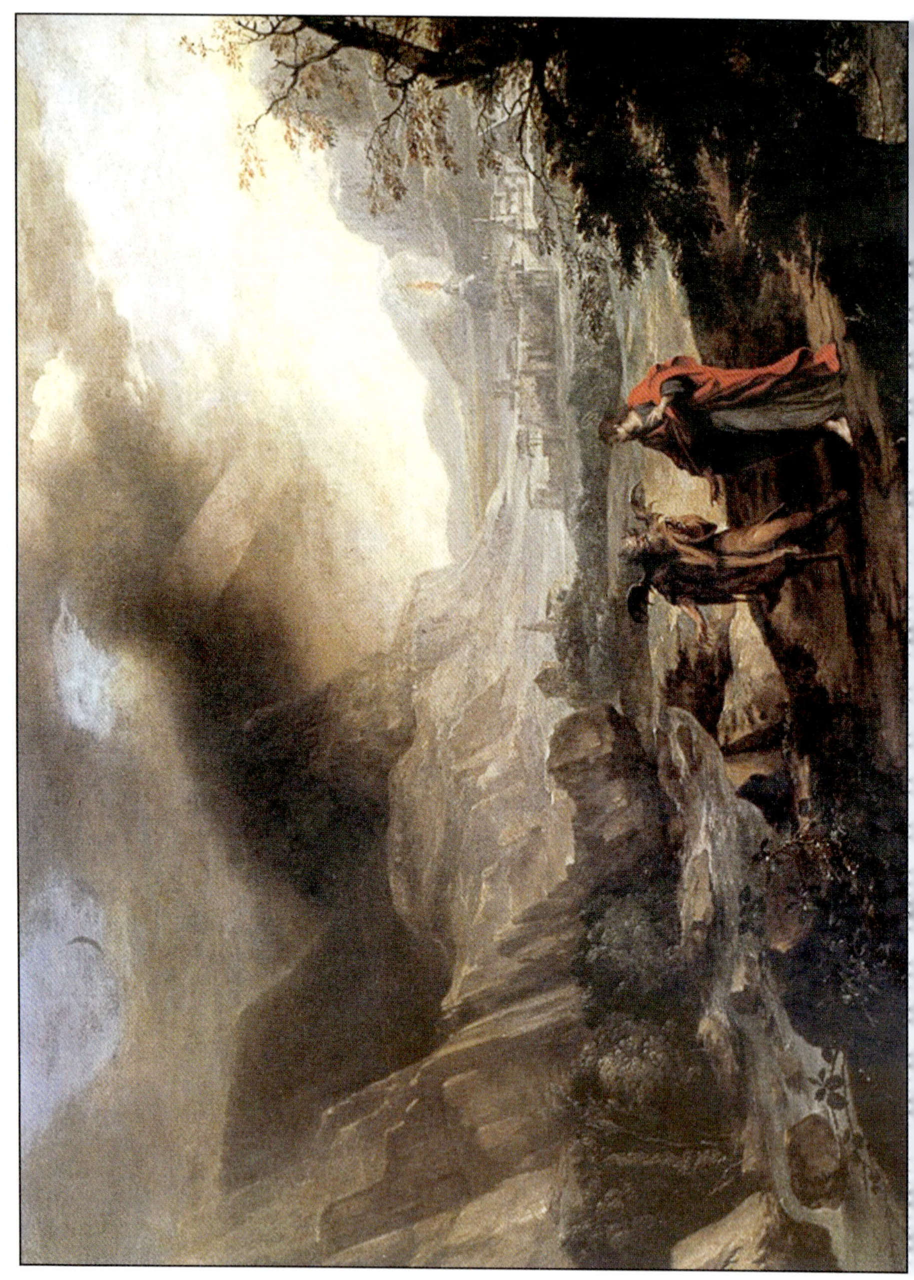

I

Temptation of Christ

THE SEASON OF Lent is a penitential time during which we pray, fast, and give alms in hopes of being transformed into the persons that God plans and desires us to become. Each week during this season, the Church presents Gospel readings that highlight our need to engage in spiritual battle, ways that Jesus can remove patterns of spiritual blindness in us, and opportunities to be raised to a higher plane of living. We know our need for transformation, so there will be many times throughout these six-plus weeks when each of us will include ourselves in the cry of the Psalmist: "Thoroughly wash away my guilt and from my sin cleanse me" (Ps. 51:4).

On the First Sunday of Lent each year, we are presented at Mass with the biblical episode that follows immediately after Our Lord's Baptism, when "Jesus was led by the Spirit into the desert to be tempted by the devil" (see Matt. 4:1–11; Mark 1:12–15; Luke 4:1–13). At the end of forty days and nights of fasting, when "he was hungry" (Matt. 4:1–2), Satan approached and began his threefold temptation. We know from this episode that the enemy's program of temptation is always the same. Engaging in *visio divina* regarding these temptations will allow us to be more aware of the temptations in our own lives, and about the better responses we are able to make.

Philips Immenraet, a Dutch painter of the Baroque period, was known primarily for landscape paintings. One of the best-known landscapes that he produced is his depiction of the *Temptation of Christ*, from 1663. This painting is unique among depictions of the desert temptation of Jesus because it includes all three of the settings in which the devil tempted Our Lord. Most other depictions focus on one single aspect of the three-part temptation, but seeing all three aspects at once allows us to ponder each successive temptation as part of a larger pattern.

In the foreground of the image, we see Jesus cloaked in the red of martyrdom. We may not realize it, but Our Lord's very journey into the desert is an act of martyrdom, as He is giving up Himself for our sanctification and salvation. The red contrasts sharply with the rest of the landscape, identifying the very countercultural nature of Jesus and His mission. Do I see myself connected to and carrying on Jesus' countercultural mission? Am I willing and ready to become subject to martyrdom for the sake of His message and mission?

Next to Jesus, we see the tempter. If the viewer knows the biblical story, it is obvious who this figure is. But from a distance, it is difficult to see this figure's demonic aspects, such as the pointed wings. He looks almost like a regular human being. This causes the viewer to examine the people around him: Are there human persons who exercise an evil influence on me? What are the ways I can know the sinister plans and effects of people with whom I interact?

The viewer can almost hear the tempter saying, as he points to the boulders on the ground, "If you are the Son of God, command that these stones become loaves of bread" (Matt. 4:3). Our Lord's response was specifically about the more necessary and lasting food that humanity needs: "One does not live by bread alone, but by every word that comes forth from the mouth of God" (Matt. 4:4). Gazing on this part of the painting allows a couple of poignant questions to resonate in one's heart: Have I let my actions be dictated more by bodily desires than by spiritual needs? Have I been more concerned with placating the physical whims of others than with their lasting spiritual good?

In the second temptation, Satan leads Jesus "to the holy city, and made him stand on the parapet of the temple" (Matt. 4:5). Jerusalem seems to be standing behind Jesus and Satan in Immenraet's painting. Above the rest of the city rises a large domed structure. While it more closely resembles the duomos of Renaissance cathedrals, this building is probably meant to be a depiction of the Jewish Temple. A pillar of fire rises from the top of the structure, which might be significant of the pillar of fire by which God led His People around the desert wilderness after the exodus from Egypt. Unlike so many people in our culture, do I put the worship of God at the center of my personal life? Have I recognized God's continual presence with His Chosen People, including the Church, which is the New Israel? Have I found myself tempted in the same way that Jesus was? Have I let pride or my power over others dictate the way that I think or act toward them?

On the left side of the painting, farther away from Jesus than the city, is a mountain wreathed in a black cloud. This is very likely meant to depict the mountain from which Satan "showed him all the kingdoms of the world in their magnificence" (Matt. 4:8). The black cloud signifies the machinations of the tempter. Dark colors in religious art are almost always significant of rejecting the light and will of God. In this biblical moment, Jesus was tempted by social notoriety and power. Looking at this part of the painting may cause the viewer to ask: Do I find myself enveloped by the black cloud of temptation? Am I tempted by social notoriety, glamor, or power? Have I allowed myself to be tempted by gathering up things and social influence for myself instead of worshiping and serving God alone (see Matt. 4:10)?

As the viewer gazes at this part of the painting, one small detail leaves a lasting impression, which makes a great conclusion. Piercing through the black cloud atop the mountain is a ray of light. That ray points almost directly at the pillar of fire rising from the Temple. The most luminous portion of the painting exists in between these two symbols of God's presence. During the Lenten season, God wants to pierce through the darkness that potentially envelops each one of us. Therefore, each of us needs to ponder precisely this question: Am I rooted in God's presence, being subject to

His light and love? Do I reject the wiles and tricks of the devil that would darken my world? That is the ultimate foundation of the growth and transformation that we all seek during Lent.

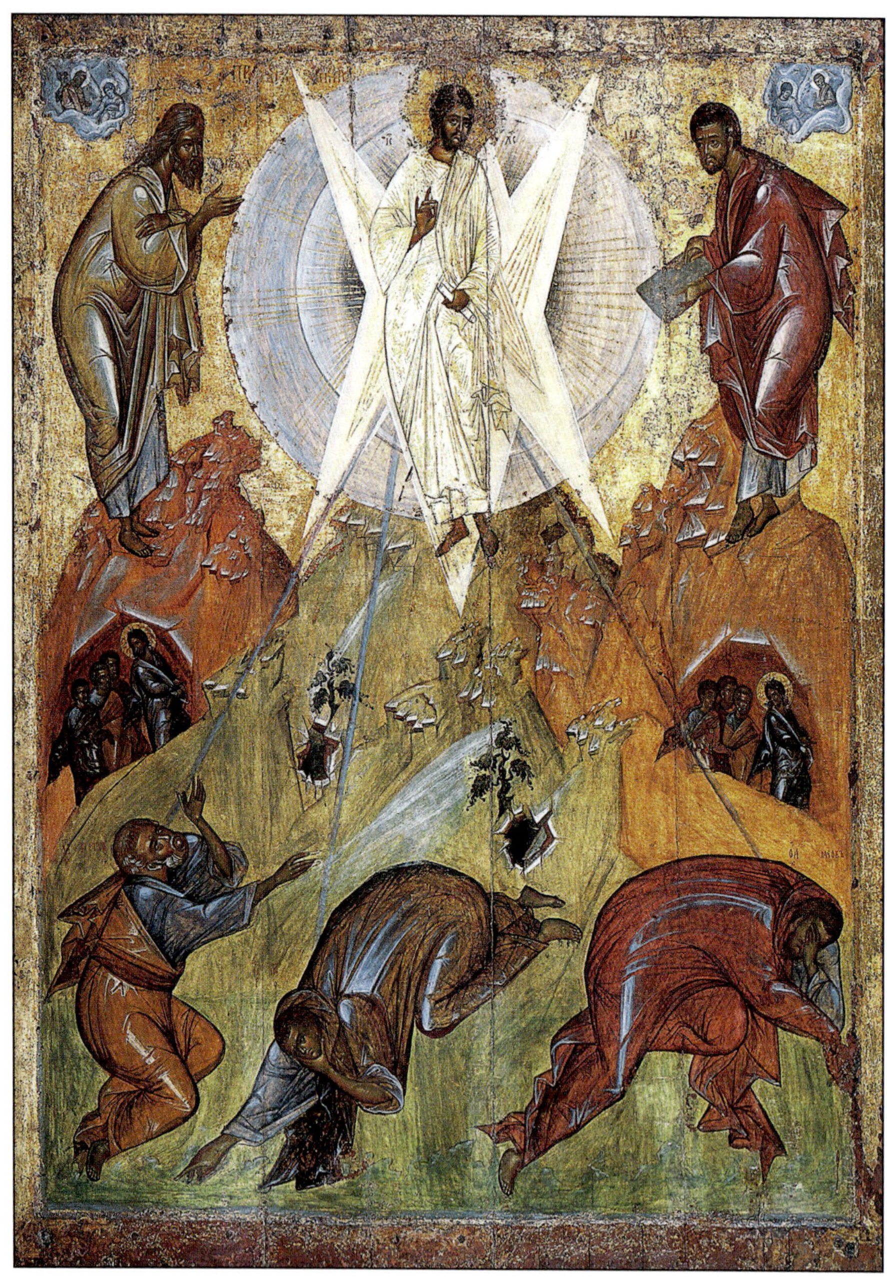

2

The Transfiguration Icon by Theophanes the Greek

ON THE SECOND Sunday of Lent each year, the faithful hear and receive the Gospel episode of the Transfiguration (see Matt. 17:1–9; Mark 9:2–10; Luke 9:28–36). Since later in this book we will look at a more traditional depiction of that event, it seems appropriate here to examine the Transfiguration through a more mystical medium that stands outside of our usual experience. The Icon of the Transfiguration by Theophanes the Greek, which was produced in Russia in the late fourteenth century, offers us a great opportunity to enter more deeply into the mystery of the Transfiguration during this season of transformation.

Eastern Christianity (the Eastern Catholic rites and Orthodox churches) employs iconography as a foundational expression of faith and spirituality. Robert L. Wilken, an esteemed historian of early Christianity, writes: "The veneration of icons is the church's most palpable way of proclaiming that God appeared in human flesh in the person of Jesus Christ. . . . What is depicted in the image of Christ is neither simply the human

Jesus nor the invisible God, but the image of God become flesh."[11] Understanding this basic truth about the incarnational principle should cause the Western Church to appreciate and benefit from this rich art form as well.

The biblical narrative tells us that Jesus took three apostles, Simon Peter, John, and James, "up a high mountain by themselves" (Matt. 17:1). This detail is reflected in small insets on both sides of Mount Tabor. On the left-hand side, the foursome walks up the mountain; and on the right-hand side, they walk downward (see Matt. 17:9). On the ascent, the apostles look quite tepid, perhaps a little unsure about what they might experience; and on the descent, they look a bit perplexed about what has just been revealed to them. Viewers, even the most ardent disciples of Jesus, might identify with both feelings. Whether during Lent or at any other time, have I been fearful of what the Lord might reveal to me? After some revelation from the Lord, has it taken me some great length of time to process and assimilate that reality?

In the top quadrant on each side of the icon, we see the two figures who were "conversing with" Jesus in the biblical scene (Matt. 17:3). On the right, Moses stands on a mountain peak and holds a book. The book certainly represents the Torah, the first five books of the Old Testament, and the mountain might be significant of Mount Sinai, from whence the Decalogue, or Ten Commandments, was revealed. Moses bows toward Jesus with crossed feet. On the left is Elijah, who represents the entire line of Old Testament prophets. The mountain on

[11] Robert L. Wilken, *The Spirit of Early Christian Thought: Seeking the Face of God* (New Haven, CT: Yale University Press, 2003), 248.

which he stands might signify Mount Carmel, which was the sight of confrontation between Elijah and the false prophets of Baal (see 1 Kings 18). Elijah bows toward Jesus with crossed arms. With each tiny detail, these figures illustrate the Christian understanding that Jesus is the culmination, the fulfillment, of the Old Testament Torah and the prophets of the Old Covenants. As a Christian, do I engage with the history and message of the Old Testament? Do I realize that, while it has been fulfilled, the Old Testament still retains its value for leading me into deeper relationship with God?

Both of these significant Old Testament figures engage with Jesus, and they point the viewer toward the One who is the focal point of this icon. The Gospel tells us that Jesus "was transfigured before them" and that "his face shone like the sun and his clothes became white as light" (Matt. 17:2). This verse of Scripture is reflected in the fact that Jesus is enveloped in white, with a burst of light behind Him, like the explosion of a star. One might ask: Do I think of Jesus as "the radiance of the glory of God" (Heb. 1:3, ESV)? Have I recognized that Jesus wants me to be transfigured by that same divine light? How can I participate in Jesus' dazzling radiance?

Behind the dazzling white mantle of Our Lord, there is a blue circle, a color and shape that are frequently used in iconography to represent heavenly realities. The fact that Jesus is at the center of this shape indicates that Eternity breaks into time in a unique and powerful way in the Transfiguration, specifically in the Incarnate Lord. From the "beloved Son" with whom the Father is well pleased (Matt. 17:5), rays of divine grace emanate to other parts of the scene, including onto Peter, James, and John. These rays indicate the transformation that can take place on the earth and in human hearts. Have I allowed God's grace to shine into my life, including in unexpected ways? Do I notice the ways that God's glory transfigures creation as well?

Another detail of the icon that indicates to us how astonishing this event was is the positions of the apostles. They are all lying prostrate. Only the apostle on the left, Simon Peter, looks toward Jesus. The apostle on the right, probably St. John, covers his face, while the apostle in the middle, St. James, looks as though he is trying to crawl away quickly. Perhaps each of us can notice all of these reactions when divine grace comes to us. Do I turn away in fear or confusion? Do I shield my eyes due to the radiant light, or in an effort not to see? Am I drawn to gaze more fully at the Lord?

One final theme is worth noting. This icon is full of brilliant colors, but all of them rest upon a background of gold. In iconography, the use of gold suggests realities that are not of this earth, those that are divine and incorruptible. In our own endeavors to live a fruitful Lent, it is necessary for us to realize that all of our activities and sacrifices flow from and are ordered toward our relationship with God. Do I see my relationship with God as the very foundation of every beautiful or challenging thing that happens in my life? Do I go about life seemingly at random, or do I allow my daily actions to arise out of my relationship with God? We should always remember that the goodness and beauty of our lives come from a real and ongoing relationship with the Lord, just as the beautiful colors of icons are built up from the gold background.[12]

The Church presents this episode to us at the beginning of this second week of Lent to reinforce the purpose of the season to us. Yes, Lent involves abnegation of self and sacrifice. Still, any and all sacrifice is ordered toward our own transfigurations, toward assimilation of the divine light that God intends to bestow on us. Let's hope, by the end of the arduous climb up the mountain of Lent, we are able to witness a miraculous transfiguration of our own bodies, minds, and souls.

[12] Some of the basic information about iconography in general and about particular themes of this icon in this essay are adapted from a commentary on ArtWay, a website dedicated to enriching human life through art. See Irena Tippett, "Mark 9:1-13 and *The Transfiguration* by Theophanes the Greek," https://www.artway.eu/posts/mark-9-1-13-and-the-transfiguration-by-theophanes-the-greek, https://artway.eu/content.php?id=1003&lang=en&action=show.

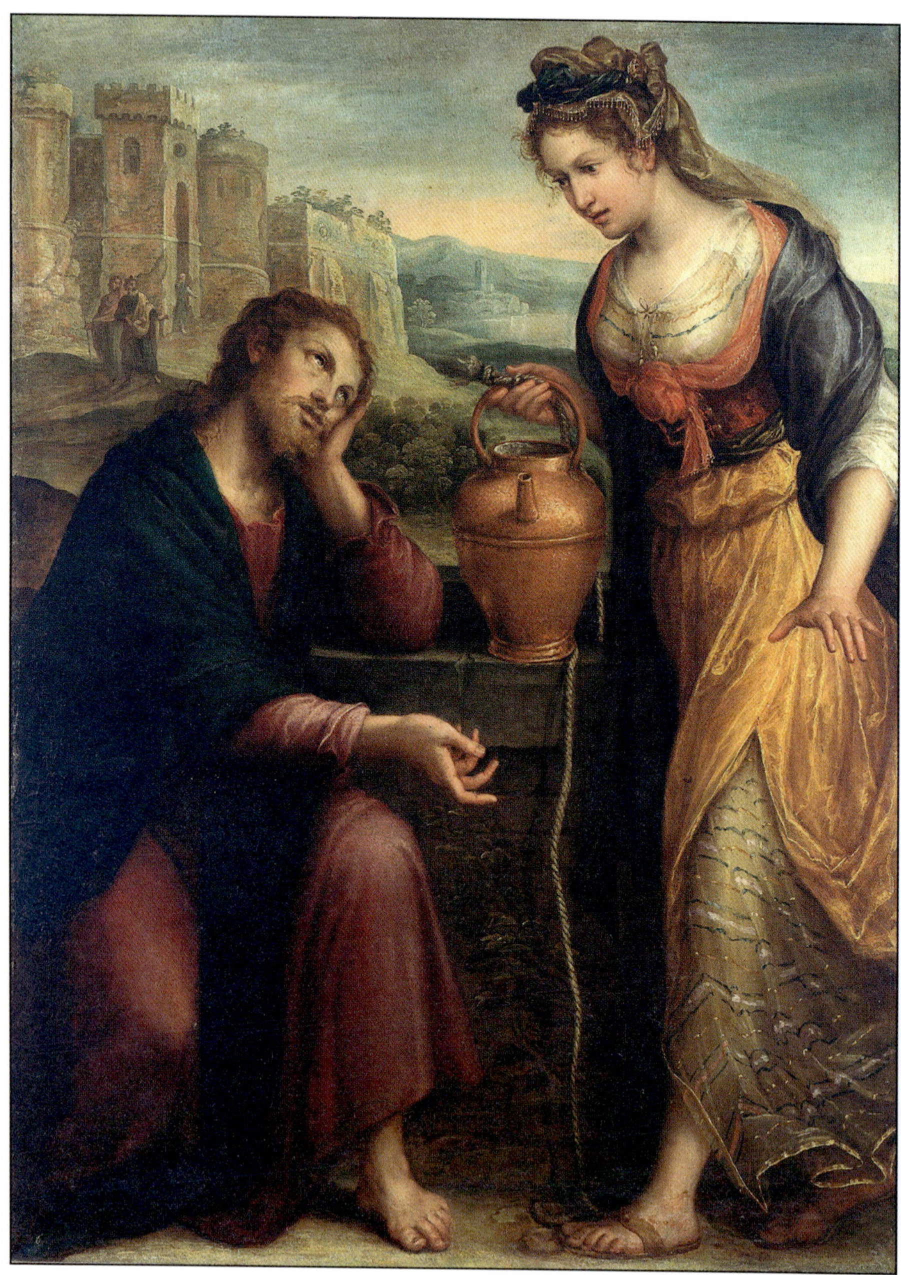

3

Christ and the Woman of Samaria

On the Third Sunday of Lent, in Year A of our Church's lectionary cycle, we hear the story of the Samaritan woman who was met by Jesus at Jacob's well (see John 4:5–42). This Gospel is used for the first scrutiny of the unbaptized catechumens who are in their final stages of preparation for initiation into the Catholic Faith because it is a story of an astonishing divine encounter, when the Messiah broke through social customs and religious norms to bring Living Water to a thirsty soul.

Christ and the Woman of Samaria is a memorable depiction of this biblical event from the early 1600s. It is memorable primarily for its artistic acumen, but it is also memorable because it was painted by a woman, Lavinia Fontana. The various aspects of the art world in Fontana's time and place were dominated almost completely by men, so she is generally regarded as the first woman to have made a career of art. Both the artist and her depiction of this biblical episode teach us to look well beyond existing norms and expectations and to look for a deeper message of truth, goodness, and beauty.

In the biblical narrative, we hear that Jesus was "tired from his journey [and] sat down there at the well" (John 4:6). In Fontana's depiction, Jesus' weariness is apparent on His face, but He still looks at the Samaritan woman whom He has come to meet in this divine appointment. Realizing this dynamic, we ask ourselves: Do I recognize that Jesus still looks at me and longs to meet me in a divine encounter, regardless of my sin or my current condition?

As we turn our eyes with Jesus toward this woman, we notice a few things about her appearance and her gestures that provide invitations for reflection. First, the woman's hair is particularly unkempt. Such a lack of styling reminds us of someone who is preoccupied with other worries and tasks. This particular detail might cause the viewer to ask: What are the worries and tasks that consume my attention? Does my attention to those things cause me to neglect other necessary tasks, or even my appearance? Is a divine encounter something I need or want in order to change this pattern?

In addition to her hair, the woman's clothing invites consideration. Her wardrobe on this day by the well is eclectic. She has on several layers, none of which match any of the others. This could indicate her preoccupation with other matters, but it might also symbolize her lack of peace and wholeness. Beyond that, we notice she has at least five layers on, with a white garment at the bottom. Perhaps this was the artist's way of signifying the original purity and wholeness the Samaritan woman had, even in her first marriage. About her clothing, we also notice that there is at least a small bit of red trim, the color of love and charity. This shows us that all persons have the potential to engage in an exchange of loving charity with others. Yet, on the Samaritan woman, it is the thinnest layer, which possibly symbolizes that her search for love was unfulfilled.

We also notice that her wardrobe stands in stark contrast to Jesus' wardrobe, which is simple and understated, yet complete and ordered. His dress garment is also completely red, indicating that He shows us the perfection of love and charity. One who gazes on the clothing in this image might reflect on what causes disorder. How is my disorder manifested on the outside? How might Jesus want to give His order and peace to me? How much of my life is an expression of Jesus Christ's love and charity?

The woman also holds a water jar, which is such an iconic image in this episode. The long rope attached to the jug might be symbolic of the many attachments that we need to discard in order to receive the Living Water that Jesus wants to give each of us. This is also the jug that the woman leaves behind when she goes back to the town to proclaim what the Lord had said and done (see John 4:28–29). What does this jug tell me about my own attachments? How deep do those attachments go in my spirit? Am I willing to leave those attachments behind for a greater joy and peace through Jesus?

The woman's left hand also makes an interesting point for reflection. Her fingers are spread wide, almost as if she is counting the number of husbands she has had in her life (see John 4:16–19). In this still picture of the scene, the viewer can almost feel the woman jerking her hand away from Jesus as if to say, "No! I will keep control of this situation!" Yet Jesus' right hand provides another notable contrast. He gestures, as if to say, "Hand over to Me the ways that those relationships have hurt you. Let Me heal your deepest wounds." This small detail of the painting allows any one of us to look into our own hearts: Am I keeping count of the things that have injured me? Do I recognize Jesus' gentle hand asking me to hand those injuries over to Him? Do I recoil from His request, thinking that I can manage and control such situations?

Two details over Jesus' shoulder elicit further reflection. First, we see a pair of apostles walking along the road, returning from their mission to buy food. They will not understand why Jesus had made this divine appointment with the woman. They will urge Jesus to eat, and Jesus will instead tell them that He has food "of which you do not know," that is, fulfilling the will and work of the heavenly Father (John 4:27, 32–34). Any disciple can continue to reflect: Am I following Jesus, completing the tasks He gives me? Are there times when I do not fully understand His intentions or methods? What helps me to understand more fully?

We also see the town that is mentioned several times in this passage, the town to which the disciples went to purchase food. More importantly, it is the town that had ostracized the woman, and it is the town to which she hurries after she leaves her jar and says to the townspeople, "Come see a man who told me everything I have done. Could he possibly be the Messiah?" (John 4:29). Are there settings in my life from which I have felt cast out, perhaps family or work settings? Is the Lord, perhaps, preparing me in any way to abandon my comfort zones and approach that setting again? What will my message be in that setting: telling of bitter grudges, or telling of the Lord's grace and healing? Am I willing to let the Divine Physician heal me by His Living Water of the bitterness and grudges that might have been or might still be in my heart?

Pondering Fontana's painting reveals to us that this encounter between Jesus and the Samaritan woman provides a basic paradigm for the whole spiritual life. All of the questions for reflection that arise from the details of this painting should be pondered throughout the year, and especially during Lent. Engaging in such a fruitful examination of conscience helps to elicit the transformation that God wants for us during this holy season.

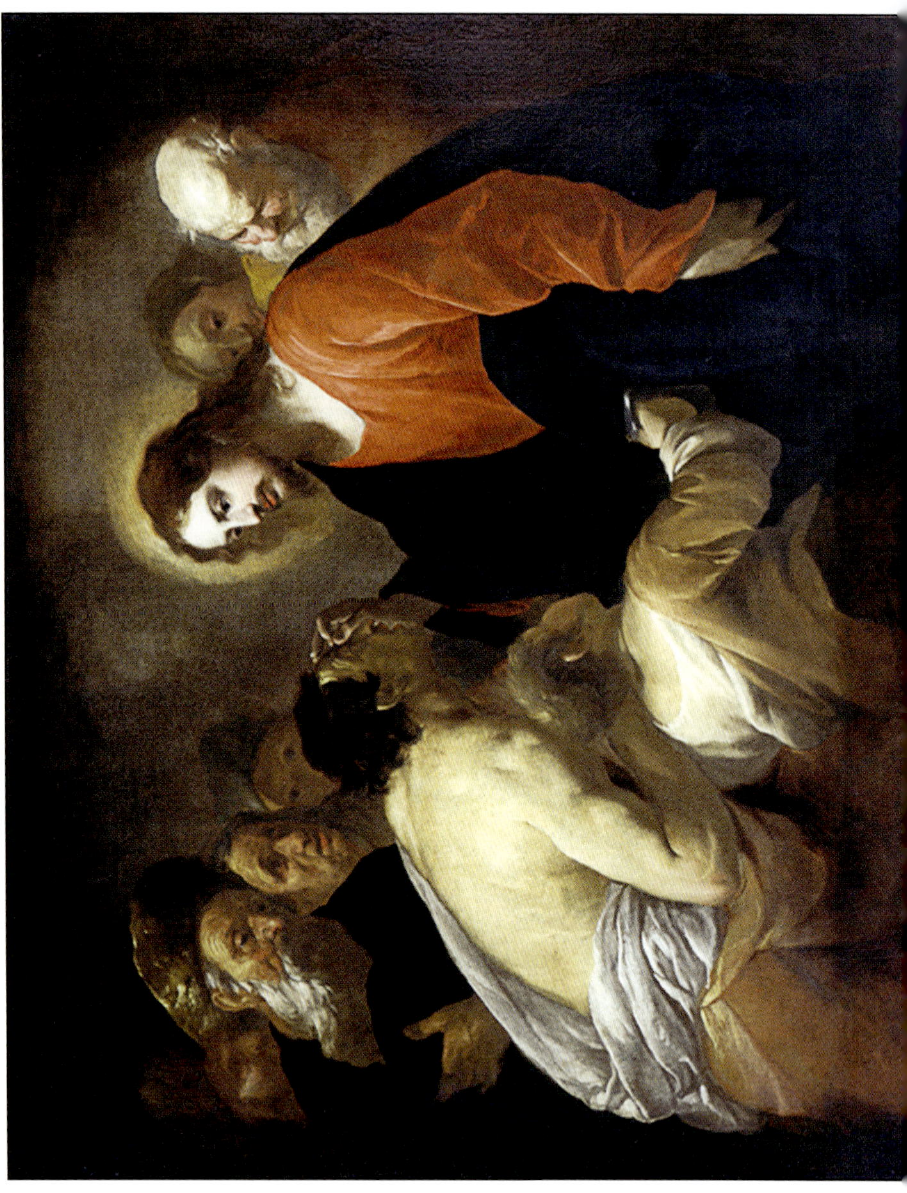

4

Healing of the Man Born Blind

Every three years, when the Church is in Year A of her lectionary cycle, on the Fourth Sunday of Lent, the faithful hear proclaimed the account of Jesus healing the man who was born blind, found in the ninth chapter of St. John's Gospel. This biblical account gives us quite a bit of detail about the way that Jesus healed the man and about the interrogation of the Pharisees in their effort to find some reason to condemn Jesus. Readers and hearers come away from this passage with a deep appreciation of Jesus as miracle-worker and healer, as well as for His method of engaging the religious establishment.

One of the most interesting artistic presentations of this event is *Healing of the Man Born Blind* by Orazio de Ferrari, an Italian artist from the seventeenth century. This painting invites the viewer to reflect on spiritual themes that are incredibly valuable for Lent. Ultimately, this piece of art helps us to know more fully why the Church presents this biblical passage to us on this specific Sunday, which is known as Laetare, or "Rejoice," Sunday.

The very first thing the viewer notices by looking at Ferrari's painting is the contrast of dark and light. The edges of the painting are dark and hazy, while light and clarity are found nearer to the center of the image. It seems as though Jesus and His action are the very source of light. This detail may cause St. Paul's exhortation from the second reading to resound in our minds: "Awake, O sleeper, and arise from the dead, and Christ will give you light" (Eph. 5:14). Lent is about moving toward the illuminated center and away from the dark fringes. This is especially apparent on Laetare Sunday, as we celebrate the fact that we are more than halfway to the light of the Resurrection. During Lent, have I sought light and clarity, especially by prayer, fasting, and almsgiving?

As in so many other images, Jesus stands at the center of the painting as its focal point. The Messiah is clad in red, creating a stark contrast from the other figures. He is also wrapped in a black cloak, which sets him apart from the rest of the figures in the image. Perhaps the artist used these details to identify the divinity, the otherness, of Jesus Christ. Still, Jesus reaches out with His human hand to touch the blind man. This gives us a remarkable opportunity to reflect on the Incarnation. True God became truly human so that He might reach out and heal our broken humanity.

Then the viewer notices the blind man. In this moment, he is hunched over, seeming quite frail. At the same time, the artist depicts him quite literally coming out of his clothes. In this passage, Jesus says, "I came into this world for judgment, so that those who do not see might see, and those who do see might become blind" (John 9:39). During the Lenten season, do I recognize how I resemble this blind man? Do I need to have my sight corrected? Am I willing to shed the comforts and protections of my life in order to receive the sight I need?

We can imagine, just before the moment captured in this painting, Jesus making the clay with His saliva that He then used to anoint the man's eyes before his sight was restored (see John 9:6). The fact that the biblical passage tells us that Jesus made clay, and the fact that the Lord's hand is so close to this man's eyes, teaches an important lesson. Yes, God wants to heal each of us and restore our sight. Still, more specifically, it is important that we know He wants to touch and heal us in a sacramental way. God provides His grace in a sacramental way, relating to us and transforming us through the material of the earth and human touch. This reflection ought to bring us to a deeper appreciation of and devotion to the sacraments. Do I recognize that God can use the material of this world to accomplish His purposes? Do I draw close to the Lord through the sacraments during Lent?

On the left-hand side, in the penumbra of the painting, stand four intriguing figures. One looks like he is critiquing Jesus' action. He could definitely be one of the Pharisees who wished to discredit Jesus as the Anointed One. A couple of the other figures look confounded and astonished. These could also be Pharisees, or they could represent the multitudes who were perplexed by Jesus' words and actions. We can reflect on both reactions and find some points for deeper meditation. Do I take on the attitude of a Pharisee, critiquing and judging words and actions that do not conform to my conception of what is right and good? Am I simply confounded and astonished by the manner that God chooses to work in my life and in the world? Do I spend enough time talking to Him about His work and His plans for me?

On the right-hand side of the image, behind Jesus, are two figures that are illuminated by slightly more light than the Pharisees. These may well represent the young man's parents, who factor into the scene. They are so afraid of the Pharisees that they simply turned the interrogation back to their son. Still, they have greater access to the light because they have witnessed the transforming miracle of their blind son receiving his sight. Like St. Thomas after the Resurrection, they have seen, so now they can believe. Has the Lord shed light on me by allowing me to witness something miraculous? When I witnessed that miracle, what was my response?

Ferrari's painting provides an incredible amount of material for reflection, even as it presents a limited number of details. The artist focuses closely on a few characters and the action of Jesus, and he brings us to a deeper devotion to the sacraments, the material means by which Our Blessed Lord reaches out and touches us. During Lent, and in every season, the faithful should make an effort to seek Jesus' light and healing. We must strive to shed life's chaotic details so that we may focus solely on Jesus' instruction. Ferrari helps viewers to recognize that Jesus does both of these things in the sacramental life of the Church. Let's take his lesson into the last weeks of Lent and into the remainder of our year.

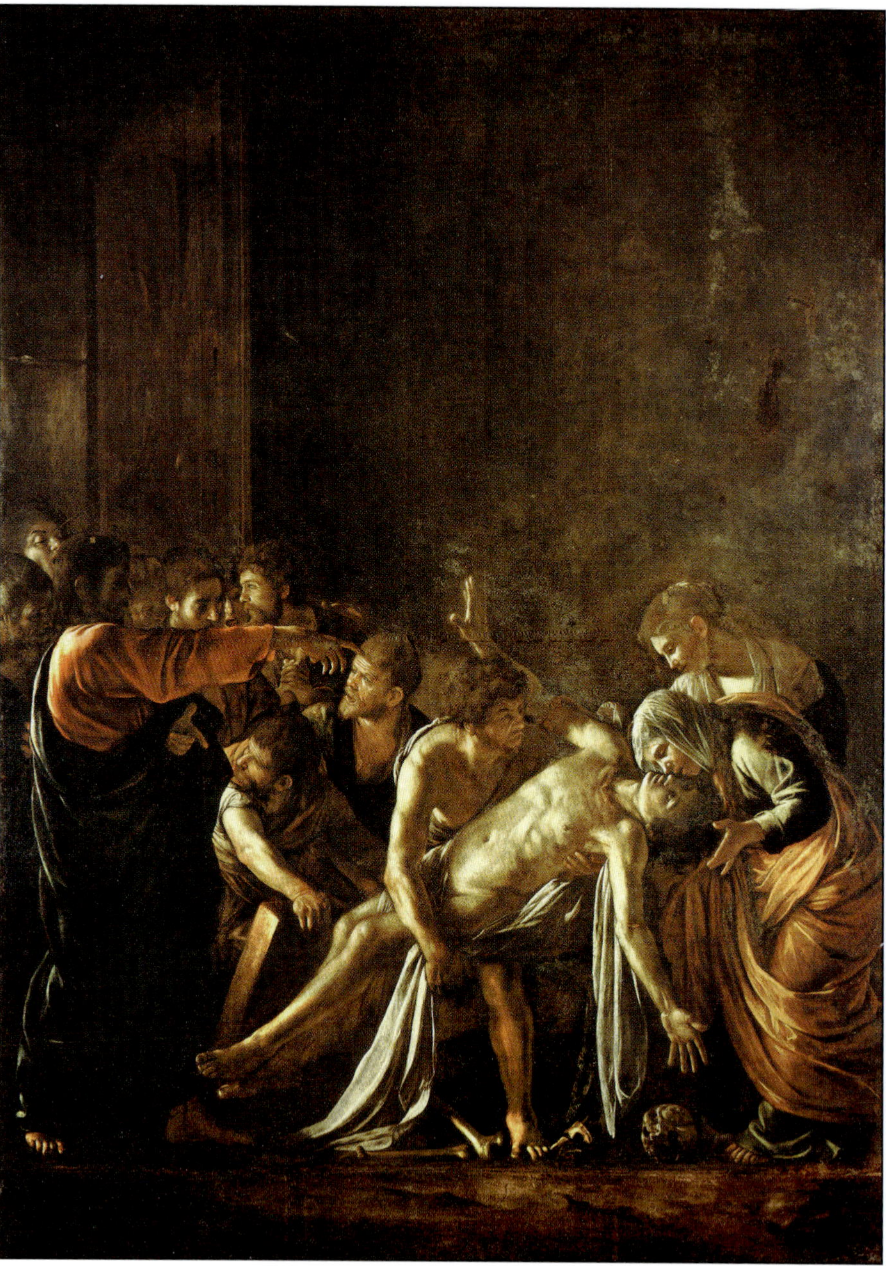

5
The Raising of Lazarus

On the Fifth Sunday of Lent, in Year A of the lectionary cycle, the Church presents to the faithful the account of Jesus raising Lazarus from the dead. Outside of the Passion narratives, this is the longest narrative of a single episode anywhere in the Gospels. It is appropriate for this particular week of the liturgical year, as we are drawing near to Jesus' Paschal Mystery, which has the potential to raise us from death to new life.

Michelangelo Caravaggio is one of the most noteworthy names in the history of Western art, as he produced some of the most recognizable paintings of the Italian Renaissance. *The Raising of Lazarus*, which Caravaggio painted in 1609, near the very end of his life, displays several of the artist's most recognizable methods and motifs. In this painting, Caravaggio masterfully captures an intense moment and gives viewers quite a bit to ponder.

Light floods this scene from the top-left corner of the painting. The figures in the scene are all illuminated by the light to a significant degree, especially those who are turned toward the light. This gives visual expression to the truth that God is the source of all light in this world, and that we become enlightened by turning toward Him. The season of Lent is about seeking and finding greater illumination, even through sacrifice and suffering. How have I turned toward the light by prayer, fasting, and almsgiving? Can I put words to specific ways that I have been enlightened?

At the left-hand edge of the painting stands Jesus Christ. His outstretched arm and His finger point toward Lazarus. Art enthusiasts, or even novices, might quickly notice that Jesus' position and gesture are a mirror image of another well-known Caravaggio painting, *The Calling of Saint Matthew*. This detail lets viewers know that Caravaggio was painting a parallel between the raising of a dead person to life and the conversion of a sinner. With his brushstrokes, Caravaggio was teaching the principle that God's greatest miracle is, in fact, the conversion of a sinner. This idea is ripe for pondering through the remainder of the Lenten season: How have I been raised to a new spiritual life? How has Jesus drawn me closer to Himself during any given day, week, or season?

On the opposite side of the painting are Mary and Martha, the sisters who "sent word" to Jesus of Lazarus's illness (John 11:3). Leading up to this moment, these women have been restlessly worried about their brother's health, which is why Mary says to Jesus, "Lord, if you had been here, my brother would not have died" (John 11:32). The viewer should pause to ponder: Are there any human or worldly situations that have occupied my attention and energy too much? How can

I learn to entrust those situations to the Lord, who holds all history in His sacred hands?

At the visual center of this scene is Lazarus, the man who was raised from the tomb. Lazarus is in a cruciform position, but at an angle. His right hand reaches toward the light, while his left hand is almost touching a skull (which seems to have been brought out of the tomb with him). This signifies that all of human life bears the possibility of divinization at the same time that it bears the possibility of eternal death. We must rely on the God-Man to provide us with the former and rescue us from the latter by His grace. As one gazes on this part of the painting, some appropriate questions come to mind: How have I reached out for the passing things of this world? How have I reached out toward the divine light that is available to me? How has that light divinized me, even in part?

We notice also the "burial bands" that had Lazarus "tied hand and foot" as well as the cloth that wrapped his face (John 11:44). In this moment, those trappings of death are nearly removed from Lazarus, but they are still apparent. This simple detail reminds us that our lives are perpetually facing the "slavery to corruption" about which St. Paul writes in his Letter to the Romans (Rom. 8:21). How are my body and mind in bondage to corruption? To what degree has God removed the proverbial burial cloths that are wrapped around me by my actions or have been wrapped around me by the actions of others?

Because Lazarus was not fully able to stand on his own at this moment, his body is held by a man while Mary, his sister, holds his head and caresses his cheek with hers. Even while Lazarus has been raised from the dead, he still relies on the support of others. This detail serves to remind viewers that each of us needs community to care for us and hold us up. Our Christian life is intended to be one of giving and receiving care and support. Each of us should reflect on where community is present in our lives. Have I helped others learn to stand more surely in the spiritual life? Have I allowed others to help me gain surer footing? Have we shown each other the love that Jesus had for Lazarus, Mary, and Martha?

Behind Jesus and Lazarus are the other witnesses of this miraculous event. Their faces bear looks on a spectrum between bewilderment and awe. Some look directly at Jesus, while others look at Lazarus. Nearly all the figures in the scene are illuminated by the source of light that comes from outside the scene. Caravaggio clearly intends to depict those "who had come to Mary and seen what he had done [and] began to believe in him" (John 11:45). This detail may cause those who reflect on this painting to ask: What has been my response when I have witnessed great miracles, especially the conversion of sinners? Am I incredulous, or does their conversion bring me to greater faith in the power of God?

In conclusion, Caravaggio's *The Raising of Lazarus* is a piece of art that superbly draws viewers into the themes of Lent, and it is an image that should be pondered as we enter into these last weeks of this penitential season. It reminds us that God, in the person of Jesus Christ, can raise the dead, even the spiritually dead, to new life. It reminds us that our whole life on this earth is a constant struggle between grasping at the vanities of this world and reaching toward the divine light that is offered from beyond this world. It reminds us of the importance of community in being lifted from and kept out of the grave of sin. If we gaze on Caravaggio's painting and remember these themes, the final days of Lent are sure to be quite fruitful.

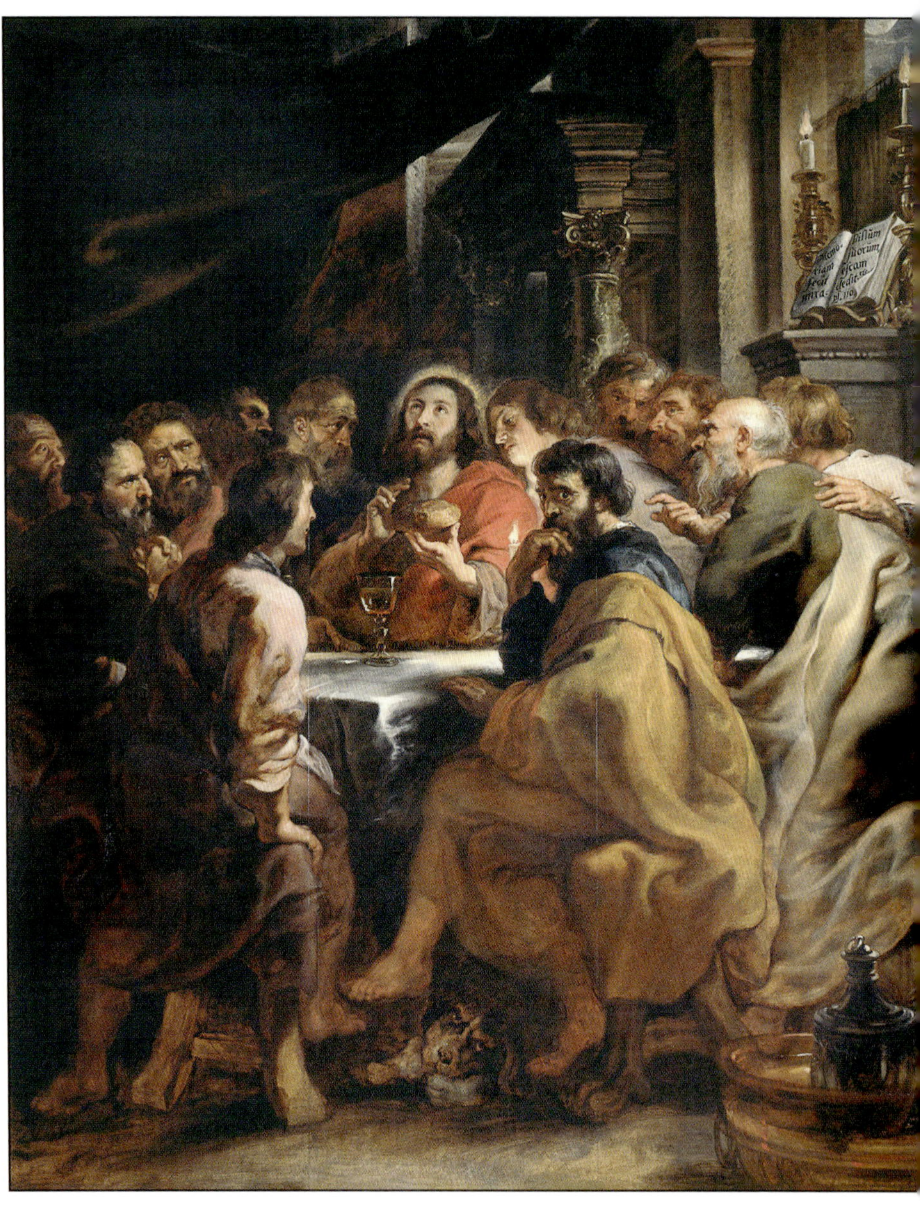

6

Last Supper

Holy Thursday is the day that we commemorate and celebrate Jesus' institution of the Eucharist, the moment that He commanded His followers to eat His Flesh and drink His Blood. Pope St. John Paul II, in his apostolic letter on the Rosary, tells us that in this event, Jesus "testifies 'to the end' his love for humanity (John 13:1), for whose salvation he will offer himself in sacrifice."[13] In this moment, the Light of the World passes on His light to others, in His own sacramental Flesh, so that they could become "the light of the world," as He had called them during the Sermon on the Mount (Matt. 5:14). It is the event in which Our Lord provided His followers the spiritual food they would need for the trials they would soon face.

Peter Paul Rubens, the Flemish Baroque artist, completed his depiction of this event, *Last Supper*, in 1630 and 1631. Originally created as part of an altarpiece for a Belgian church,

[13] Pope St. John Paul II, apostolic letter *Rosarium Virginis Mariae* (October 16, 2002), no. 21.

this painting offers several captivating details about the Eucharist. It especially provides a rich opportunity to reflect on the theme of light, specifically our capacity to live as the light of the world.

Jesus, of course, is the focal point of this painting. His position and His gaze bring the viewer into a palpable sense of close proximity in this moment. As the Messiah turns His eyes heavenward, we can almost hear His high priestly prayer recorded in John 17: "Father, the hour has come; glorify your Son that the Son may glorify you" (John 17:1, ESV). This depiction of an intensely intimate moment ought to provide a font for ongoing relationship with the Father, whose every action is intended to draw close to humanity.

Jesus holds a small loaf of bread in His left hand above a chalice of wine. These are the species that were transformed at that First Eucharist and continue to be transformed at each Mass throughout history. Our Lord's right hand is raised in the gesture of a blessing, by which He provided the prototypical gesture and action that transformed the bread and wine into His very Body and Blood, and which has been extended by the sacred priesthood for all subsequent generations. When a viewer sees this detail, the words of institution over the bread and chalice quickly come into our minds and hearts (see Luke 22:19–20). Rubens's depiction of the species and the sacred action ought to bring each of us to a deeper devotion to the liturgy as well as the sacred vessels and offerings that are presented to God for transformation.

Another important detail augments this point, but it might escape us without close examination. As Jesus raises His eyes to

Heaven and holds the bread in His hand, a shaft of light pierces downward onto Him and the eucharistic species. This is surely representative of two things: the action of the Holy Spirit to transform the bread and wine (*epiclesis*); and the relationship of intense love that exists within the Trinity. Again, the viewer is brought into this intimate exchange of love and power. The viewer is now capable of taking on the light and power that are available through relationship with Jesus.

Continuing with the motif of light, we notice a single candle in the middle of the table, next to Jesus' left arm. This candle emits light that illuminates the bread and the apostles closest to Jesus. This could be significant of the candles employed during liturgies, but it also holds a more general connotation. The Light that comes into our midst spreads out and transforms those who draw near. Am I in a habit of drawing near to the Light?

The apostles gathered around the eucharistic table extend the motifs of light and heavenly relationship even further. Some, like St. John the Evangelist, bear a greater degree of illumination. Others of them match the Lord's gaze heavenward. Some of them, while illuminated and looking at Jesus, remain perplexed, as if they are skeptical of what He says. Where do I fit in here? Do I allow myself, my life, to be illuminated by the light that Jesus brings? Do I look at Jesus skeptically, doubting the full truth and implication of what He says? Do I follow His gaze?

The most notable figure around the table is Judas, who looks away from the Lord and directly at the viewer. Unlike the other apostles, he has turned away from the Light provided by this eucharistic moment. He bites his knuckle while bearing a look of grave concern on his face, as if to ask the viewer if he should continue with his sinister plan. There is so much about this depiction of the betrayer in this moment that aids an examination of conscience. Have I deliberately removed myself from the Eucharist and other sacraments? Even if I have attended Mass each week, have my attentions been on something less important, something away from the altar? Have I persisted in sinful decisions out of pride, envy, or greed? What causes me to turn away from the light that Our Blessed Lord emits?

Another interesting detail is the dog that rests under Judas's feet. Throughout the history of art, dogs have typically represented fidelity and loyalty. Yet in this painting, even the dog bears a cynical look on his face. Perhaps Rubens included this figure in a stroke of cynicism and irony, intending the dog to represent greed or envy, those loyalties of Judas that led him to betray Jesus for thirty pieces of silver. Each person who looks at this painting ought to ponder his own fidelity and loyalty: Am I faithful and loyal to my Lord, His Church, and the vocational call He has given to me? Am I greedy or envious of others' victories and benefits?

Finally, at the top right of the painting, there is an open book whose inscription reads, "Memoriam fecit mirabilium suorum, escam dedit, etc." This is the Latin text of the first words of Psalm 110:4–5 in the Vulgate Bible (Psalm 111:4–5 in newer English translations): "He has caused his wondrous works to be remembered; the Lord is gracious and merciful. He provides food for those who fear him; he remembers his covenant forever" (ESV). The inclusion of this passage is clearly meant to show the viewer that this event is the fulfillment of the Old Covenants. It is by the Eucharist that the "wondrous works" of the Lord are remembered; the Eucharist is the food Our Blessed Lord provides for "those who fear him." The viewer will also quickly notice the two lit candles atop large candelabras, which continue the theme of light in this painting. The Word of God, the Bible, is another source of light that emanates from the Divine Source.

Peter Paul Rubens has therefore employed light in a number of ways to help viewers understand Jesus as the Light of the World. His *Last Supper* draws viewers into the intimacy of the Trinity and the Church at worship, which are the sources of that light. It also creates an opportunity for each of us to examine the dispositions and actions that might take us away from the Lord. Ultimately, a painting like this one, and like the Blessed Sacrament it depicts, helps us to become the light that each of us is called to be.

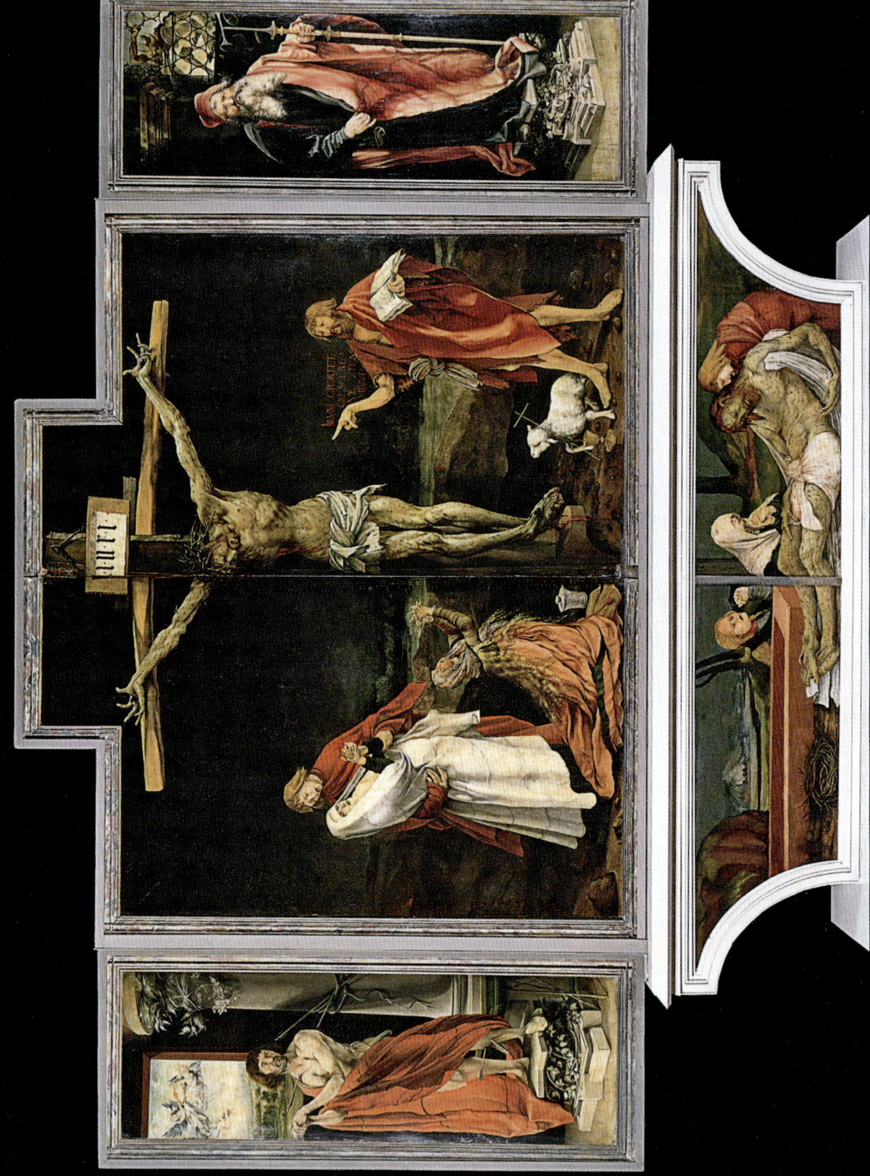

7
The Isenheim Altarpiece

Holy Week provides an opportunity for a very real and personal participation in Jesus' Paschal Mystery. By these celebrations, the actions that effect our salvation are re-presented to the faithful. Particularly in the unique Good Friday liturgy, when we venerate the Cross and enter and leave church in complete silence, we are plunged downward in Jesus' death so that we can be raised upward with Him in the Resurrection.

Between 1512 and 1516, Nikolaus Hagenauer, a sculptor, and Matthias Grünewald, a painter, crafted an altarpiece for a monastery in Isenheim, France. The whole altarpiece depicts several scenes from the Gospels and the history of the Church. The best-known depiction, which is the focus of this essay, is the painting at the center of the altarpiece when it is closed fully. Grünewald uses this central painting and the predella (the altarpiece's base) below it to bring viewers more deeply into the pain, sorrow, mystery, and power of Holy Week. This painting leads us to the glory of Easter even as it presents those events in a downward trajectory.

At the top center of the first triptych, the viewer readily notices the crucified Christ. This part of the painting allows us to enter more deeply into the mystery of Jesus' Passion and Crucifixion. The Messiah is clearly suffering as His emaciated Body hangs contorted and bleeding. The events of Holy Week are, in fact, a painful experience of suffering and loss. The Passion and death of Jesus are altogether different from ordinary human experience, and they are at the same time both harrowing and beautiful. Each of us might ask: Have I allowed myself to feel the movements of Holy Week on a visceral level, beyond the intellectual? Do I understand that pain and suffering can be doorways to beautiful joy?

One other detail about the crucified Christ is significant. We notice that His skin is covered with black spots. This gives expression to the Black Plague, which led to a difficult time of great suffering in European history. The monks at this monastery in Isenheim had tended to plague victims centuries prior. Aside from that historical reality, this detail also gives artistic expression to the fact that sin is a spiritual and moral plague. The artist clearly intended to echo St. Paul's words in his Second Letter to the Corinthians: "For our sake he made him to be sin who knew no sin, so that in him we might become the righteousness of God" (2 Cor. 5:21, ESV). Jesus has borne our plague of sin and death so we have the opportunity to live.

On the right of the scene is St. John the Baptist, who wears a red garment symbolic of his martyrdom at the hands of Herod the tetrarch (see Matt. 14:1–12). In his left hand, the Baptist holds an open book, quite likely meant to reference the prophets of the Old Covenants, of whom the Baptist was last in line. He points directly to the Crucified Lord, as was his mission according to the Gospels. At John's feet is a lamb whose blood drips into a chalice. Clearly, each of these details is meant to remind viewers that John was the one who exclaimed, "Behold, the Lamb of God, who takes away the sin of the world" (John 1:29). Do I allow St. John's words to continually resound in my mind and heart, especially during Holy Week? Do those words remind me that Jesus, the "lamb led to slaughter" (Isa. 53:7), is the source and author of my salvation?

On the left side of the scene, we first notice the woman draped in white. This is Mary, Jesus' mother, whose garment signifies her purity. Her hands clasped in prayer, and her eyes closed, she leans back as though she may have fainted in sorrow. This image has the potential to bring viewers to a deeper devotion to Our Lady of Sorrows. Do I find a deeper understanding and connection as I walk the movements of Holy Week with the sorrowful mother?

The figure who holds Jesus' sorrowful mother is St. John the Evangelist, the only apostle who remained with the Messiah throughout His Passion. That John holds and protects Mary is symbolic of Jesus' words from the Cross to those two: "Woman, behold, your son!" and "Behold, your mother!" The apostle himself commented, "And from that hour the disciple took her into his home" (John 19:26–27). Have I beheld the purity, charity, and devotion of the Blessed Mother? Do I realize that her devotion for her divine Son is the same devotion she has for me? Have I brought her habit of pondering things in her heart into my own soul (see Luke 2:51)?

The final figure depicted here is Mary Magdalene, who also remained with Jesus throughout His execution. She wears a pink garment while she kneels at the foot of the Cross, and her hands are folded in prayer. Her garment is a hybrid color of the red and white that others wear in the scene because she not only took up a life of purity after her conversion but also took up a life of radical devotion, which may have caused her to face a social martyrdom. Am I like Mary Magdalene as a disciple? Do I have radical devotion to Jesus because of the way that He has transformed me, as He transformed Magdalene?

Below the Crucifixion scene is the predella of the altarpiece. This particular predella depicts the Lamentation of Jesus, the moment when the crucified Lord was laid in His tomb. This motif was common in early Renaissance painting. Viewing this part of the altarpiece leads us to reflect on the time of waiting, anxiety, and anticipation that the Blessed Mother and other disciples experienced on the day following the Crucifixion. How do I observe the Lamentation? Do I keep Holy Saturday as a time of solemn prayer and preparation?

While the altarpiece painting presents the Paschal Mystery of Jesus in visual form and serves as an ornamentation to foster the very worship of the Church, it is the altar itself, which would have stood below the predella depicting the Lamentation, that makes the fitting conclusion of this downward trajectory through the Sacred Triduum. For it is the altar, whether in Jerusalem or Isenheim or anywhere else, upon which the Eucharistic Lord, the Risen Christ, is made truly present in the *Panis Angelicus*, the bread of angels. The Eucharist is the culmination of what Grünewald painted. It is the pinnacle of the Paschal Mystery, the ultimate Easter reality, for it is the Flesh of the Resurrected Jesus, offered to the faithful for the redemption of our own bodies and souls.

PART IV

The Art of Easter

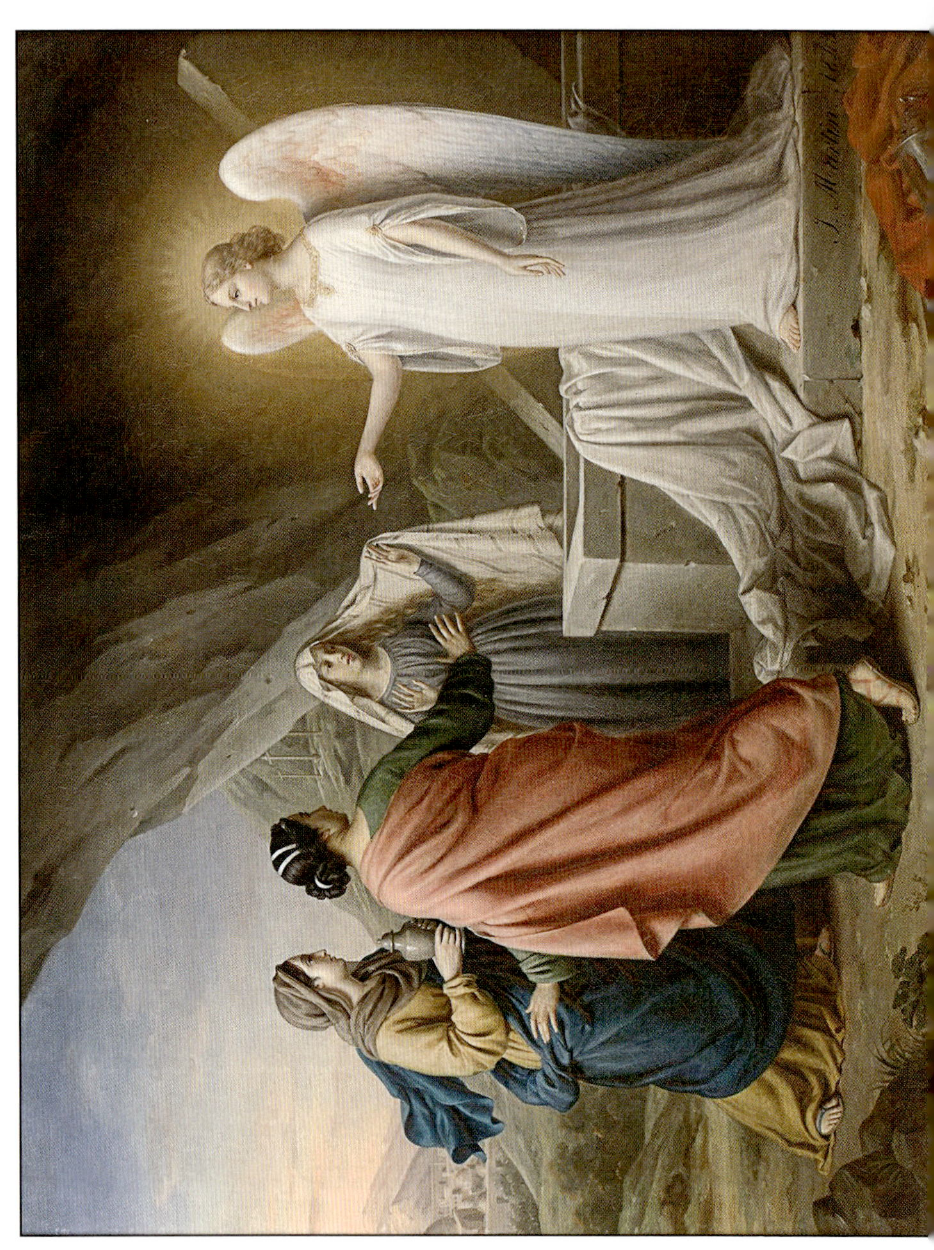

I

The Three Women at the Tomb of Christ

We have come through Lent and the Sacred Triduum to the holy season of Easter. We celebrate this triumph of Our Blessed Lord over death first for a full octave (eight days) and then for six more weeks following! This is the longest season of our Church's liturgical year, and rightfully so, because the faithful *need* more than one day, more than one week, to unpack the profound mystery that has shattered our conception of life.

Sacred art, especially that of the last five centuries, is replete with images of Jesus rising from the tomb on Easter morning. Those familiar with art history might quickly think of paintings by Francesca, Titian, Tintoretto, El Greco, Carl Bloch, or Peter Paul Rubens that deal with this event. While these great works of art offer abundant opportunities for deeper meditation, here we will take time to examine art that is a bit more peripheral. In 1843, a French artist named Irma Martin provided her own visual interpretation of the Gospel authors' accounts of Easter morning in her painting *The Three Women at the Tomb of Christ*, in which she invites viewers to ponder

Christ's Resurrection from the perspective of the three women who had gone to the tomb to anoint Jesus' Body after the lawful sabbath rest (see Luke 23:55–56).

The viewer quickly notices the setting of this scene. This tomb has a large opening, an opening that would have necessitated "a huge stone" to cover it (Matt. 27:60). From the viewer's vantage point, through this hole in the tomb, the artist connects the movements of Holy Week and the Paschal Triduum. At the very left-hand edge of the painting, we see the holy city of Jerusalem, the site of Jesus' last week of teachings and the site of the New Passover meal He had recently celebrated with His apostles. Between the city and the tomb, up a steep hill barely two hundred yards from the rock-hewn sepulcher, stand three empty crosses. This hill is Golgotha. As we reflect on Holy Week and ruminate on these details, we can ask ourselves: Have I come to appreciate the movements of Holy Week and the Paschal Triduum? Do I enter into these celebrations anticipating the glory of the Risen Lord?

Inside the tomb, viewers are greeted by the angel whose "appearance was like lightning and his clothing was white as snow" (Matt. 28:3). The angel extends his hand to the women, and he speaks the message he was sent to convey from God: "Do not be afraid! I know that you are seeking Jesus the crucified. He is not here, for he has been raised just as he said. Come and see the place where he lay" (Matt. 28:5–6). Has a message of truth, even something I might not have expected, come to me from the Lord and any of His messengers? Have there been times that such a message has been both shocking and beautiful, perhaps at the same time?

The angel gestures toward the empty sarcophagus at the center of the scene. Its lid is shoved to the side at an angle, showing that it has been quickly dislodged. An empty burial cloth lies over the side of the sarcophagus, falling to the floor. Do I recognize the mysterious reality that the Resurrection is? Have I spent time letting the reality of the empty tomb sink into my mind and heart? Have I tried to view all the mysteries of my own life in light of Jesus' Crucifixion and His Resurrection, which are both shocking and beautiful?

Just between the sarcophagus and the opening of the tomb are the three women who are the subjects of the painting. St. Mark tells us that these three women are "Mary Magdalene, Mary the mother of James, and Salome." Although we do not know exactly which woman each figure is, each is in a posture that is valuable for meditation.

The woman at the left of the scene holds a jar. This jar is certainly meant to depict the "spices so that they might go and anoint him" (Mark 16:1). Perhaps the spice that she holds is myrrh, which was commonly used in the ancient world to anoint bodies for burial. While it certainly is not specified in the scriptural texts, it would have rich meaning if this were the jar of myrrh that was presented by the Magi at Jesus' Nativity, some three decades earlier. What do I bring to anoint Jesus as Savior and Lord?

The second woman is turned toward the viewer. Her gaze is fixed on the empty tomb, and she raises her right hand like a student prepared to ask a question. The look on her face gives powerful expression to St. Luke's comment about the thought these women had in this moment: "And they remembered his words" (Luke 24:8). Have I taken time to read and reflect on the words of Sacred Scripture, especially the Gospels, and realize how they are fulfilled in the Resurrection? Can I take time to read more Scripture (for the first time or again) during the Easter season, reading everything in the light of the Risen Lord?

The third woman has her back turned toward the viewer and makes visible the group's response to the instructions of the angel (see Matt. 28:7 and Mark 16:7). This woman seems as though she is already moving away from the tomb and heading back to Jerusalem. She flings her arms open wide, as if to say, "Enough! I can't figure this out, but I know what I've been told to do." Her position allows the viewer to ponder the whole group's response as recorded in the Gospels: fear, trembling, astonishment, and great joy (see Matt. 28:8 and Mark 16:8). These details might cause any one of us to question: Do I have the disposition of going quickly to tell others about mysterious and miraculous realities? Do I respond in faith to God's directions, even when I don't quite understand fully?

Finally, in the bottom-right-hand corner, on the floor, lies a piece of red cloth with a lantern on top of it. This could be the artist's way of presenting the detail given by St. Matthew: "And behold, there was a great earthquake.... The guards were shaken with fear of him and became like dead men" (Matt. 28:2, 4). The Roman soldiers who were guarding the tomb (see Matt. 27:62–66) were overcome by the sheer power of the Resurrection. Like these soldiers, have I been overcome, even shocked, by the reality and power of God? Am I willing to have my perspective changed, like the centurion who witnessed the Crucifixion and then exclaimed, "Truly, this was the Son of God!" (Matt. 27:54)?

Martin's painting faithfully and cleverly captures the details that we read in the Gospel accounts. It allows us to see the events of Easter morning from a different perspective than is commonly presented as we meditate on the mystery and power of the Resurrection. Let us pray that our meditation, our silence listening for the Lord's truth, impels us quickly on a mission to tell of His glory, just like these women on Easter morning.

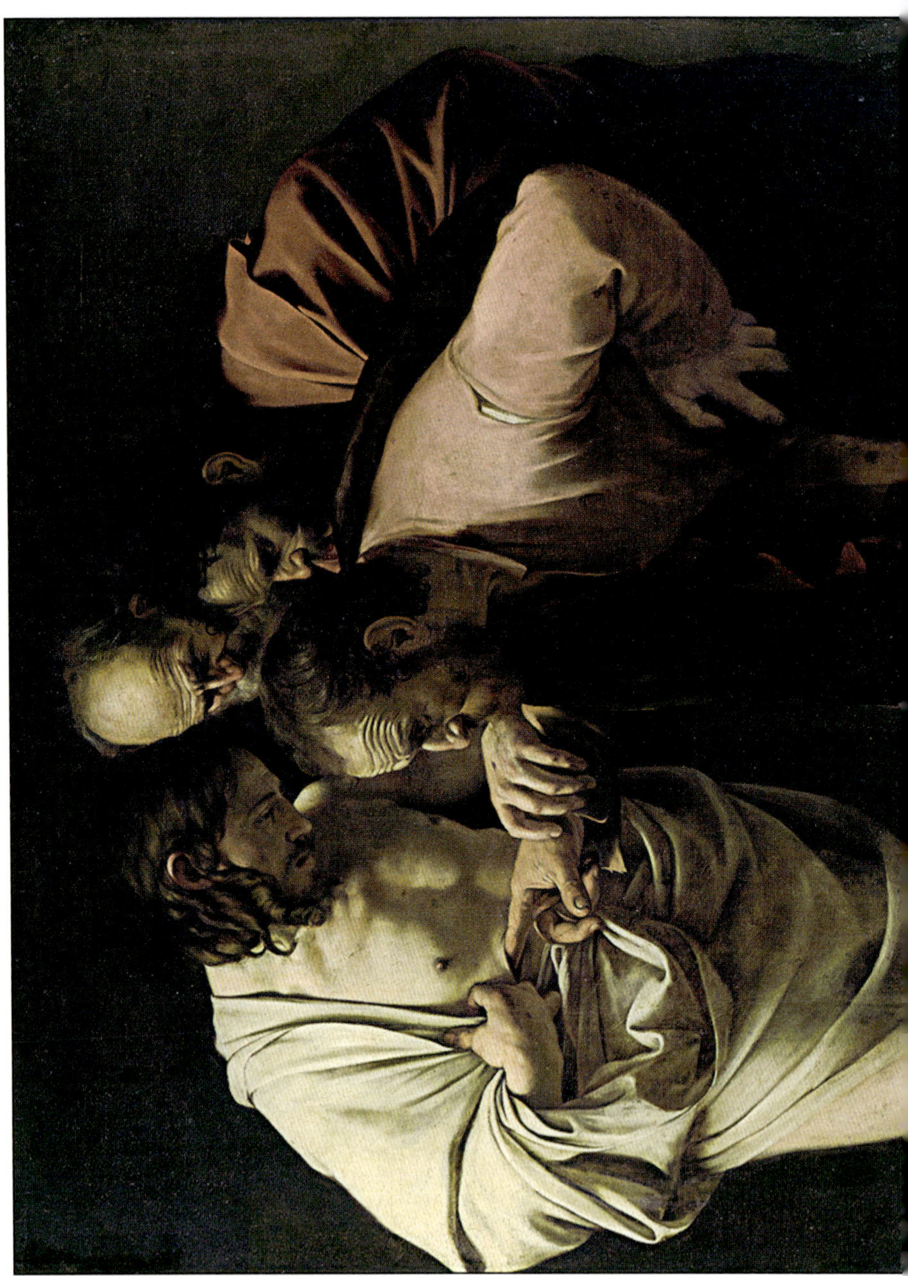

2

The Incredulity of Saint Thomas

EACH YEAR ON the Second Sunday of Easter (known as Divine Mercy Sunday since the Great Jubilee Year 2000), the Church proclaims the Gospel passage in which the apostle Thomas, known to posterity as "Doubting Thomas," sees and touches Jesus' scars from the Crucifixion (see John 20:19–31). Without a doubt, this Gospel episode has a great impact on the faithful, perhaps because we realize just how much we are actually like the incredulous apostle.

In the first years of the seventeenth century (1601 and 1602), at the tail end of the Italian Renaissance, Michelangelo Caravaggio painted another of his well-known masterpieces, *The Incredulity of Saint Thomas*. Using his recognizable *chiaroscuro* technique, Caravaggio brings the viewer to the very center of this mystical moment. By being so close to the personal exchange of Jesus and His apostle, and through limiting the surrounding details, this painting creates a powerful spiritual statement and a rich opportunity for deep meditation.

The *chiaroscuro* technique, which employs light and shadow for deeper artistic effect, is the most prominent characteristic as the viewer approaches this painting. Throughout Caravaggio's work, and in this painting particularly, this technique causes the viewer to reflect on the presence of spiritual light and darkness. What are the sources of light in my life? Is the darkness quickly encroaching on the light, or is the light shining forth and overcoming surrounding darkness?

The background of this painting is completely dark, which serves two purposes. First, the dark background allows the viewer to be drawn into an intensely intimate moment in the life of a disciple and the Church. Second, the dark background allows the viewer to generalize and bring the scene to his or her own life. It causes the viewer to question: Have there been times in my life when I have obstinately refused to believe Jesus' revelation without tangible evidence?

At the forefront of the painting, we notice St. Thomas, hunched over, looking intently, and placing his finger in the lance wound in Jesus' side. It is hard to see, but Thomas is wearing a dark-colored cloak.[14] At the moment captured in this painting, the cloak is already halfway removed, and it seems to be falling off the rest of the way. This ought to remind us of the tandem work, the unity, of reason and faith in arriving at a full understanding and appreciation of truth. Thomas, as a stalwart of empiricism, has only shed half the cloak of darkness. Even Jesus says as much to him: "Have you come to believe because you have seen me? Blessed are those who have not seen and have believed" (John 20:29).

[14] This detail can be seen more easily in the brighter "Ecclesiastical Version" of the painting from 1601.

The look on Thomas's face brings us even more deeply into this astonishing moment. His eyes pop open wide, and his brow is furrowed in surprise, creating lots of wrinkles. The viewer is almost able to hear his reaction recorded by St. John the Evangelist: "My Lord and my God!" (John 20:28). Is this my reaction when I see Jesus, especially in the Eucharist? Do I fall to my knees in Adoration? Do I echo St. Thomas's exclamation at the elevation of the Host at Mass?

We notice another hand guiding the doubter's hand. Jesus told Thomas to "bring your hand and put it into my side" (John 20:27). The artist makes visible the Lord's command and His desire to be known fully. This detail, which seems so obvious and simple, reminds us that it is the Lord's grace that opens up our relationship with Him, that leads us to knowledge of Himself and of the universe. Do I allow Jesus to direct me toward the evidence and answers I seek? Do I realize that all knowledge is meant to lead me closer to Him?

While considering the position of Thomas's hand, it is easy to notice both of Jesus' hands and the scarred wounds of the Crucifixion they bore. In the words of Ven. Fulton Sheen, these are "the unmistakable scars of battle against sin and evil," which Our Blessed Lord bore "to prove that love was stronger than death."[15] Have I spent time meditating on the scars of Christ? Do I realize that Jesus looks at me *through* His scars? Do I also bear wounds and scars of my own? Do these scars affect my relationships with others? Are the scars I bear able to help me foster deeper relationships with and love for others?

[15] Sheen, *Life of Christ*, 610.

We also notice that Our Lord is the most luminous figure of the four depicted. While He does not seem to be the source of light in this painting, the fact that He is the brightest of all the characters pictured captures our Catholic belief that Jesus is the recapitulation of all God's saving words and actions throughout the history of the Old Covenants (see CCC 430).

Behind Jesus and Thomas are two other figures. Based on the biblical text, we can assume that these are two of the apostles gathered in that Upper Room. Still, the fact that they are not specifically identified provides two avenues for deeper reflection. The first avenue is that these figures represent any one of us as a disciple of the Lord. Do we watch as other disciples try to meet Jesus and grow in relationship with Him? Are we impacted positively or negatively by their efforts?

The second avenue for consideration is that these men stand for the visible Church. Throughout the centuries, the Church has stood close by but in the background, watching and approving the probing work undertaken to advance empirical knowledge of God and the universe through theology, philosophy, and the natural sciences. Do I trust the judgment of the Church when it comes to the definition of truth? Do I believe that the Church can help me find truth in either the natural or the spiritual realms?

As we recall this memorable post-Resurrection event during the Easter season, let's all hope that, with St. Thomas, we can learn to discover and appreciate the saving wounds of Jesus. Let's also hope for the divine grace that heals all wounds. Let's lift up and celebrate the diligent work that the Church has always done to foster greater knowledge of all scientific, historical, and theological truth. Most of all, let's hope to remain where Jesus wants to bring us, to His wounded side and to His Sacred Heart.

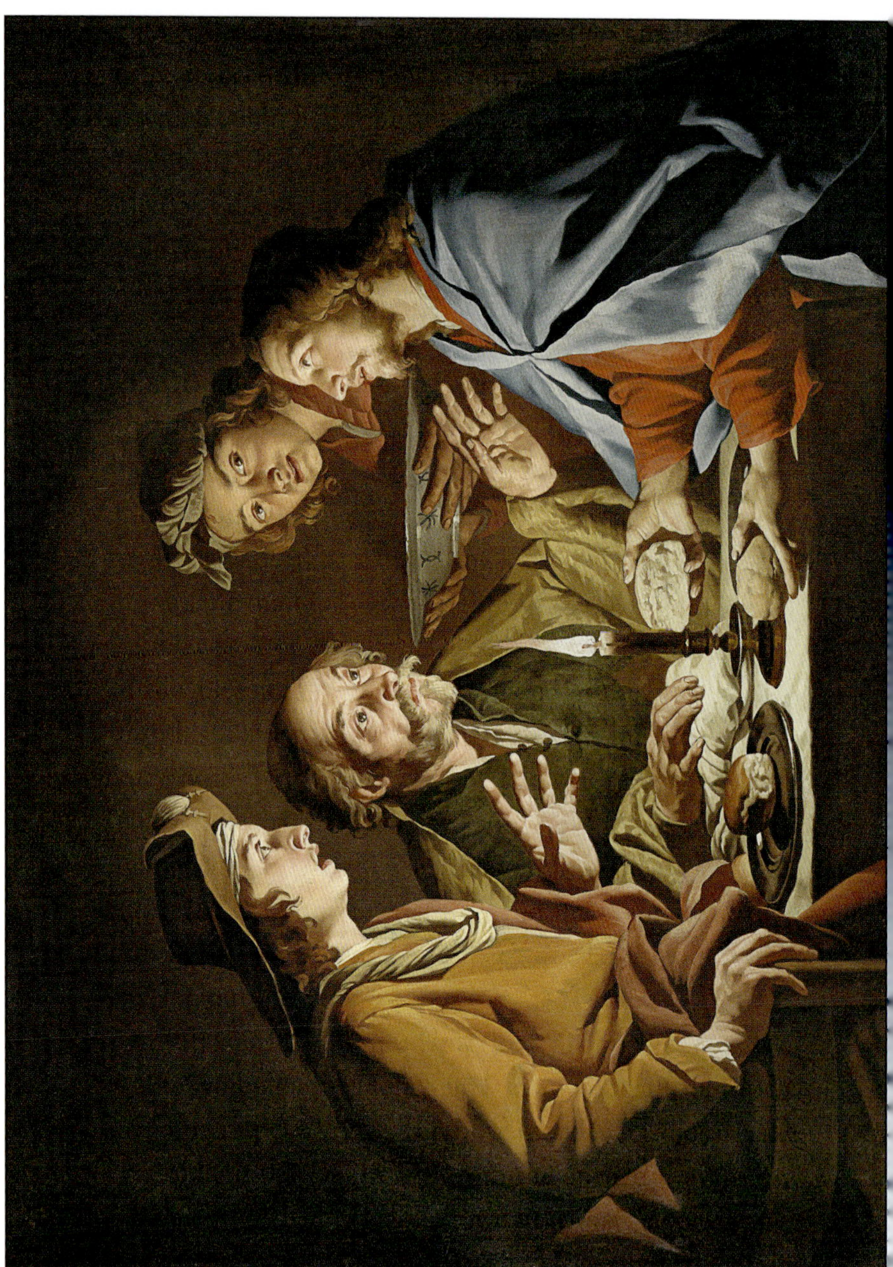

3

Supper at Emmaus

IN YEAR A of the Church's liturgical calendar, the Gospel reading for the Third Sunday of Easter allows the faithful to hear about the two disciples who were walking to Emmaus and experienced a miraculous meal at their destination (see Luke 24:13–35). As we listen to the whole story, we get a glimpse into the conversation that took place between the two disciples and their mysterious Interlocutor. We also learn of their sorrow because "we were hoping that [Jesus] would be the one to redeem Israel" (Luke 24:21). We hear of the greatest Bible study in history (see Luke 24:27) and, finally, of the intimate meal that led to an amazing revelation. This journey-turned-pilgrimage is truly one of the greatest Easter episodes in the Gospels.

In the 1630s, Matthias Stom, a Dutch painter influenced by students of Caravaggio, painted several versions of *Supper at Emmaus* in which he depicted the miraculous meal in this biblical passage. Each of the versions has unique and memorable details, but here we will focus on the version that is currently housed at the Museo Nacional Thyssen-Bornemisza in Madrid, on which Stom worked for more than half a decade.

In this painting, Stom employs two techniques that Caravaggio used with great effect. First, Stom uses a dark background, which creates a sense of deep intimacy: it is as though this dinner table with these four figures is the only place in the world at this moment. Second, Stom employs the *chiaroscuro* technique that Caravaggio mastered, giving texture to the scene by the deep contrast of dark and light. The artist's use of these two techniques reveals that great art stands in continuity with other great works and artists.

The light for this painting's *chiaroscuro* seems to be emitted from a single candle in the middle of the table. This candle causes viewers to recall the powerful words of the prologue of St. John's Gospel: "The light shines in the darkness, and the darkness has not overcome it" (John 1:5, ESV). This visual theme also has potential to remind the viewer of the Paschal candle at the Easter Vigil Mass, which brings the light of the Risen Christ into the darkened church. One who gazes at this painting might ask questions related to light: How has the Light of the World illuminated the dark, shadowy areas of my life? Has the Lord provided moments of light that have allowed me to know more about who He is and what He has planned for me?

This painting brings viewers directly into the moment when "their eyes were opened and they recognized him," just before "he vanished from their sight" (Luke 24:31). We see Jesus holding two halves of the small loaf of bread in His hands.

This opens up a consideration of profound and glorious moments in which we have received a deeper understanding about Jesus in the Eucharist. Has the Lord remained hidden from my sight for a time, perhaps during a very sad time, only to reveal Himself more fully later? How did I respond when He made that revelation?

The three men who are in this room with Jesus are uniquely instructive. The two men seated at the table with Jesus are Cleopas and the other unnamed disciple. In this version of the painting, the artist presents the two disciples as widely variant in age: one is quite a bit older, and one is quite young. This detail depicts the reality of the Church, which is made up of people of every stage of life. Am I able to recognize that every baptized person has something unique and special to contribute to the life of the Church, regardless of age or any other physical or social condition?

The third figure at the meal is an outsider, someone who was not part of the pilgrimage from Jerusalem and the conversation with the hidden Jesus. Perhaps he is a servant at the inn where they intended to lodge. In any case, the artist depicts him as looking on with great intrigue, even awe, in this moment. This simple detail causes the viewer to remember that there are many "outsiders" who know of Jesus, who long for the grace that He offers, and who have the potential to be great evangelists. This detail also reminds us that it is up to us, the faithful, to reach out and bring these people into the fold of the one, holy, catholic, and apostolic Church. Have I been part of the apostolic mission of the Church, reaching out to provide others with an opportunity to come closer to Jesus?

The postures of both seated disciples, and the looks on their faces, are also significant for reflection. As the older disciple realizes the identity of this Mysterious Guest, he reaches out to touch the One who has revealed Himself. He looks at Jesus in a way that says, “I want a deeper relationship with Jesus, my Lord, and I want to understand more.” Gazing at this painting might cause the viewer to ponder: Have I longed for deeper intimacy with Jesus? Have I reached out to try to touch Him through Eucharistic Adoration, the study of Sacred Scripture, or ministry to the sick?

The young disciple at the left of the scene is aghast as he realizes the miracle that has just occurred and what it means about Jesus’ identity. At this very moment, he begins to stand up. This is the artist’s way of depicting his transition from being downcast to becoming an apostle and evangelist. Immediately, both disciples “set out at once” for a return trip to Jerusalem to share what they had experienced. When I relate to Jesus in the Eucharist, either at Mass or at Adoration, am I impelled to mission? To whom do I go to tell the Good News I have encountered? Do I realize that this is supposed to be a reality after *every* Mass and period of Adoration?

As we reflect on Stom’s painting, and as we move through the Easter season, let’s remember these lessons that Our Blessed Lord desires to teach us in our own time and place. Let’s reach out to Jesus and ask Him to draw us more deeply into His life and love, especially through the Breaking of the Bread. Let’s be ready to go out on mission, proclaiming what we have seen, especially to those who are intrigued to hear the Gospel. In these ways, we will become the disciples and apostles that the Lord intends us to be.

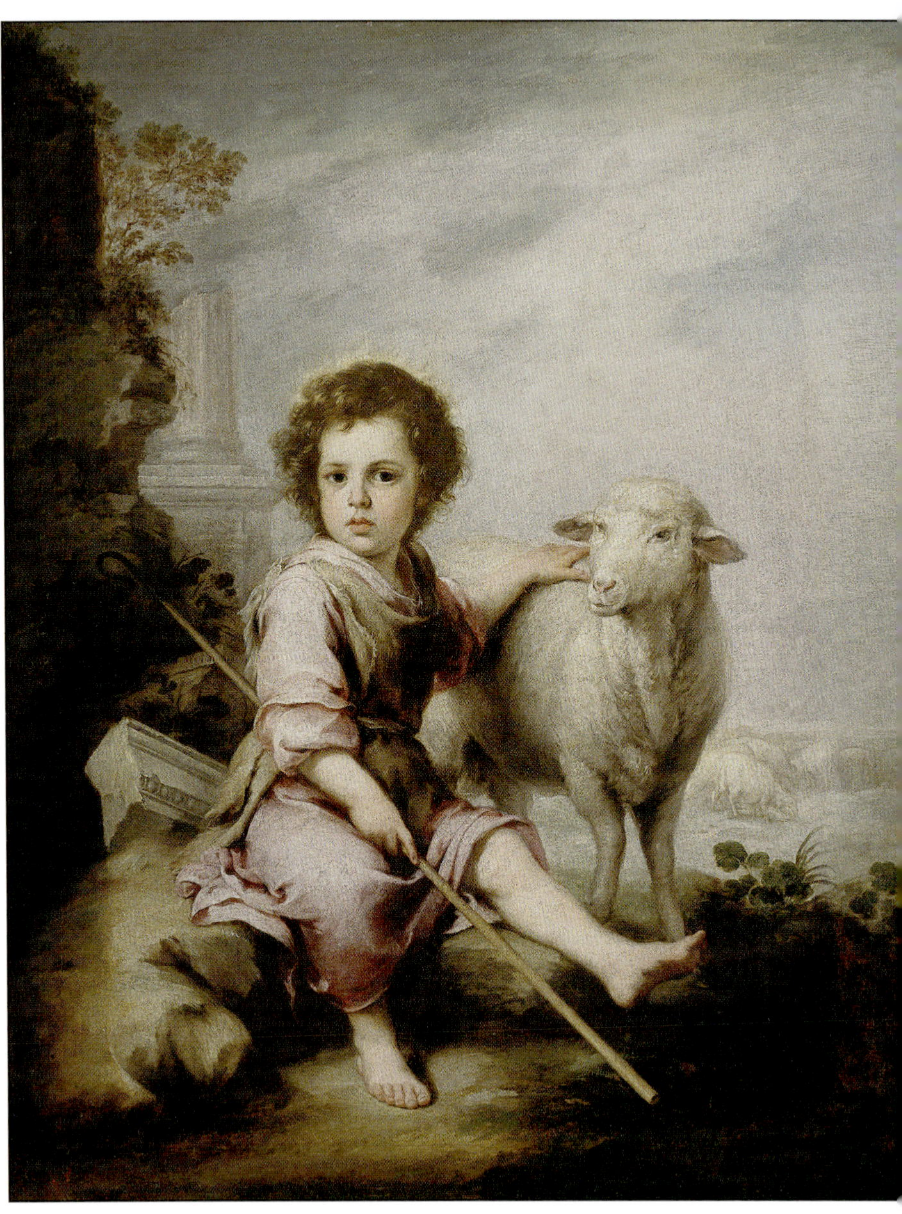

4

The Good Shepherd

On the Fourth Sunday of Easter in each liturgical cycle, the Church presents to the faithful a portion of Jesus' Good Shepherd discourse, which is recorded in the tenth chapter of St. John's Gospel (see John 10:1–10, 11–18, 27–30). This passage is one of the most beloved in all of Sacred Scripture, and it is especially crucial as we teach our Faith to our children and help them to grow in their spirituality. It also reminds the faithful of how Jesus is both gatherer and defender of those who hear His voice and follow Him.

Bartolomé Esteban Murillo, one of the great artists of the Baroque era in Europe, produced several memorable depictions of Jesus as the Good Shepherd. The one that he made around 1660, which hangs today in the Prado Museum in Madrid, is perhaps the most famous and memorable. This version contains some important details that depict Jesus as Gatherer and Defender, the quintessential tasks of a shepherd.

As a viewer approaches this painting, the very first thing he notices is that Jesus is depicted as a child. It is no coincidence that Murillo decided to portray Christ as a child, since there are multiple moments throughout the Gospel narratives when Jesus mentions children (see Matt. 18:3–4 and Luke 9:46–48). Additionally, in this passage, Jesus tells His audience, "I came so that they might have life and have it more abundantly" (John 10:10). Who has life more abundantly than a joyful child? Have I let myself become more childlike to experience the joy that Jesus wants me to have?

This Child's gaze pierces into the viewer's soul and might cause the viewer to think about his or her own connection with the Good Shepherd. With His eyes, He says, "I want a deeper relationship with you. I want to gather you to myself and protect you." Being drawn in by His gaze will allow us to "recognize his voice" more clearly (John 10:4). Am I willing to meet the Good Shepherd's gaze and hear His voice?

The Christ Child holds a staff, the quintessential tool of a shepherd, under His right arm. This staff is a tool for both gathering, by the crook, and defending. What are the tools that Jesus uses to gather people into relationship with Him through His Church? What are ways that He defends His flock? What has He done to gather and defend me, personally?

The Shepherd's left hand rests on a sheep. The look on His face conveys a stark seriousness. By His look, and by the placement of His hand, the Good Shepherd says, "My Father, who has given them to me, is greater than all, and no one can take them out of the Father's hand. The Father and I are one" (John 10:29–30). As I gaze on this painting, can I recall times when I have felt the protective hand of the Lord in my life? Have I ever thought of myself as a feeble, even helpless sheep? Has the Lord been tender to me in the midst of such feebleness?

Behind the Shepherd and His one sheep, on the right-hand side of the painting, is a herd of sheep. This causes the viewer, first, to think about Jesus' teaching in the Good Shepherd discourse: "I have other sheep that do not belong to this fold. These also I must lead, and they will hear my voice, and there will be one flock, one shepherd" (John 10:16). Do I realize that God wants every person as a part of His sheepfold? Even as a sheep, am I willing and ready to help other sheep come into the one flock of the Lord, the Church? How can I do this in my own life?

It also seems that Murillo has used the distant flock as a visual statement of Jesus' well-known parable of the lost sheep and to remind us of the ninety-nine that remained faithful (see Matt. 18:10–14 and Luke 15:1–7). The sheep that is right next to the Good Shepherd, caressed by His hand, therefore also represents the "one sinner who repents" and who is the cause of more rejoicing than "ninety-nine righteous persons" (Luke 15:7, ESV). Am I willing to view myself as a lost sheep? Am I willing and ready to allow the Lord to change my sinful ways and lead me back to the flock?

Finally, just behind the Shepherd Child is part of a destroyed building and, farther back, a broken and toppled column. This is one of the most significant details of the painting, and it seems that Murillo uses these images to convey that Jesus and His teachings have conquered ancient paganism, especially that of the Roman Empire: "All who came [before me] are thieves and robbers; but the sheep did not listen to them.... A thief comes only to steal and slaughter and destroy" (John 10:8, 10). The serenity of the Good Shepherd who gathers, defends, and bestows abundant life stands in stark contrast to the wreckage and ruins. Have there been areas of my life that the Lord has had to topple and overcome? Have I been drawn into the fullness of truth, slowly discarding my old ways of seeking wealth, pleasure, power, or honor so that I might seek the Lord instead?

While Murillo's painting offers relatively few details, the ones that he does offer are quite poignant. Through them all, the viewer can come to know Jesus more deeply as Gatherer and Defender, the One who protects the whole flock while still searching out the lost sheep who are astray, and he can reflect on his or her own relationship to the Good Shepherd and to the One True Flock, the Church. Growing in this awareness will allow each of us to appreciate more fully the depth of the Paschal Mystery and the Easter season.

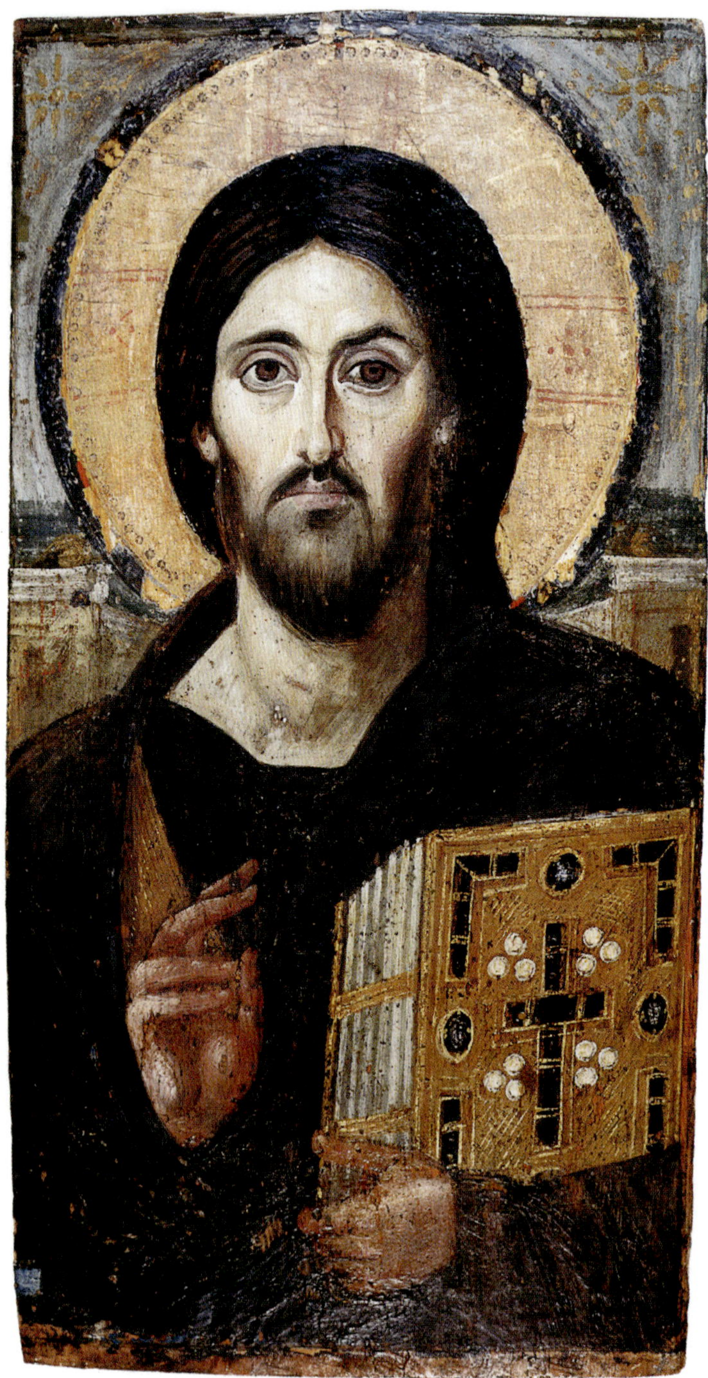

5

Icon of Christ Pantocrator

During the Fifth and Sixth Sundays of Easter, the Church proclaims Gospel passages from Jesus' Last Supper discourse. In Year A of the Church's liturgical calendar, the Gospel passages for these two Sundays come from the fourteenth chapter of John's Gospel (see John 14:1–12, 15–21). Some of Jesus' best-known axioms, as well as some of His most significant promises, appear in this chapter as Jesus shares with His apostles and disciples the contours of their sharing in the life of grace that will be available to them after the Resurrection.

There is a dearth of art relating specifically to this discourse in the Western Christian tradition, perhaps because of the mysterious and mystical nature of Jesus' words as recorded by St. John. And so we must look outside of the Western artistic tradition and again ponder icons as part of *visio divina*. Icons present a more mystical and mysterious style of art. They give viewers a specific window into the divine mystery and lead us into meditative and contemplative prayer.

One common icon of Jesus is Christ Pantocrator (translated as "Christ, Ruler of All" or "Christ, Almighty"). There are many, many well-known versions of Christ Pantocrator around the world, especially in Eastern churches (the Church of the Holy Sepulcher in Jerusalem, for example). The oldest and one of the best-known of these icons resides at the foot of Mount Sinai at the Eastern Orthodox Monastery of St. Catherine. It has been fostering meditation on Jesus, the Almighty, since at least the 600s A.D.

This icon depicts Jesus alone. This is eminently appropriate for the Last Supper discourse. The five chapters that record this episode consist of nearly a complete monologue. There are only a few interlocutions from the apostles to whom He was speaking. Jesus and His words are the focal point of the description by St. John, and He is the focal point by the iconographer of St. Catherine's Monastery.

The fact that Jesus is alone in the icon provides the viewer an opportunity to ponder the Lord's statements about Himself at greater length. "I will come back again and take you to myself," He says. "I am the way and the truth and the life. No one comes to the Father except through me" (John 14:3, 6). How often have I allowed myself to focus solely on Jesus? How often have I considered that He intends to speak these words directly to me and desires me to focus on nothing other than my relationship with Him?

One of the realities that comes through strongly in Jesus' discourse, especially in John 14, is the union of Jesus Christ and the Heavenly Father, the First and Second Persons of the Trinity. Jesus answers Philip's request to be shown the Father:

"If you know me, then you will also know my Father.... Whoever has seen me has seen the Father.... Do you not believe that I am in the Father and the Father is in me?... Believe me that I am in the Father and the Father is in me" (John 14:7, 9–11). Have I explored the truth that Jesus is, in fact, the Perfect Revelation of the Heavenly Father, with whom He shares the fullness of the Divine Nature? Do I realize that when I relate to Jesus, I am brought closer to the Heavenly Father as well?

This particular icon also invites us to reflect on another important theological reality. Looking closely, the viewer will notice that the two halves of Jesus' face are subtly distinct. This detail offers us the opportunity to reflect on the fact that Jesus was, at the same time, both fully divine and fully human, a phenomenon known as the hypostatic union. Indeed, when we examine the Person of Jesus Christ closely, whether through sacred art, Sacred Scripture, or the sacraments, we come to know Him in both His divinity and His humanity. When we come to know Him in both His natures, we come to appreciate the distinct ways that He manifests each. Have I sought deeper understanding of the Person of Jesus Christ, in both His humanity and divinity?

In His left arm, Jesus cradles a book. Presumably, this book is the Sacred Scriptures, perhaps specifically the Gospels. There are multiple ways that Jesus' words in this discourse relate to the Sacred Scriptures. In the Mass readings for the Sixth Sunday of Easter in Year A of the Church's calendar, we hear Jesus tell the faithful, "If you love me, you will keep my commandments.... Whoever has my commandments and observes them is the one who loves me" (John 14:15, 21). It is important for us to realize that the story of God's covenantal love, which is revealed in Sacred Scripture, comes along with commandments, rules, and regulations for how to honor our relationship with Him. We learn to keep the commandments in two parts: first, in learning what those commandments are (specifically, the Ten Commandments, or Decalogue, and the Beatitudes); second, by understanding the ways that faithful disciples have responded previously. In order to be in deeper relationship with Jesus, have I immersed myself in the story of Sacred Scripture? Because I love Him and want to keep my relationship with Him, have I learned God's commandments? Have I become convinced that my actions need to align with His commands and desires for my life?

Finally, the viewer notices that Jesus raises His right hand in blessing. This is a visible depiction of two promises that Jesus made during His discourse. First, He promised to send us the Holy Spirit: "And I will ask the Father, and he will give you another Advocate to be with you always, the Spirit of truth, which the world cannot accept" (John 14:16–17). Second, He told the apostles and us, "I am the way and the truth and the life.... I live and you will live" (John 14:6, 19). The blessing of Jesus Christ is something mysterious, something that we cannot fully understand. Yet His blessing sends forth the Holy Spirit and bestows on us a first taste of the divine life in which we are meant to live and flourish. Do I seek out Jesus' blessing, especially through the ordained ministers of the Church? Do

I deprive myself of that gift through my own actions, such as by leaving Mass before the final blessing?

The icon of Christ Pantocrator from St. Catherine's Monastery in Sinai is a window into the deep, eternal Mystery that is intended for all humanity to know and ponder. By pondering this icon, we are able to dive more deeply into that Mystery and grow in our relationship with the God-Man, Jesus Christ. In deepening our relationship with Our Blessed Lord, we are taught to turn our minds and hearts toward Him so that we may we know His Truth, travel His Way, and share in the Abundant Life that He lives.

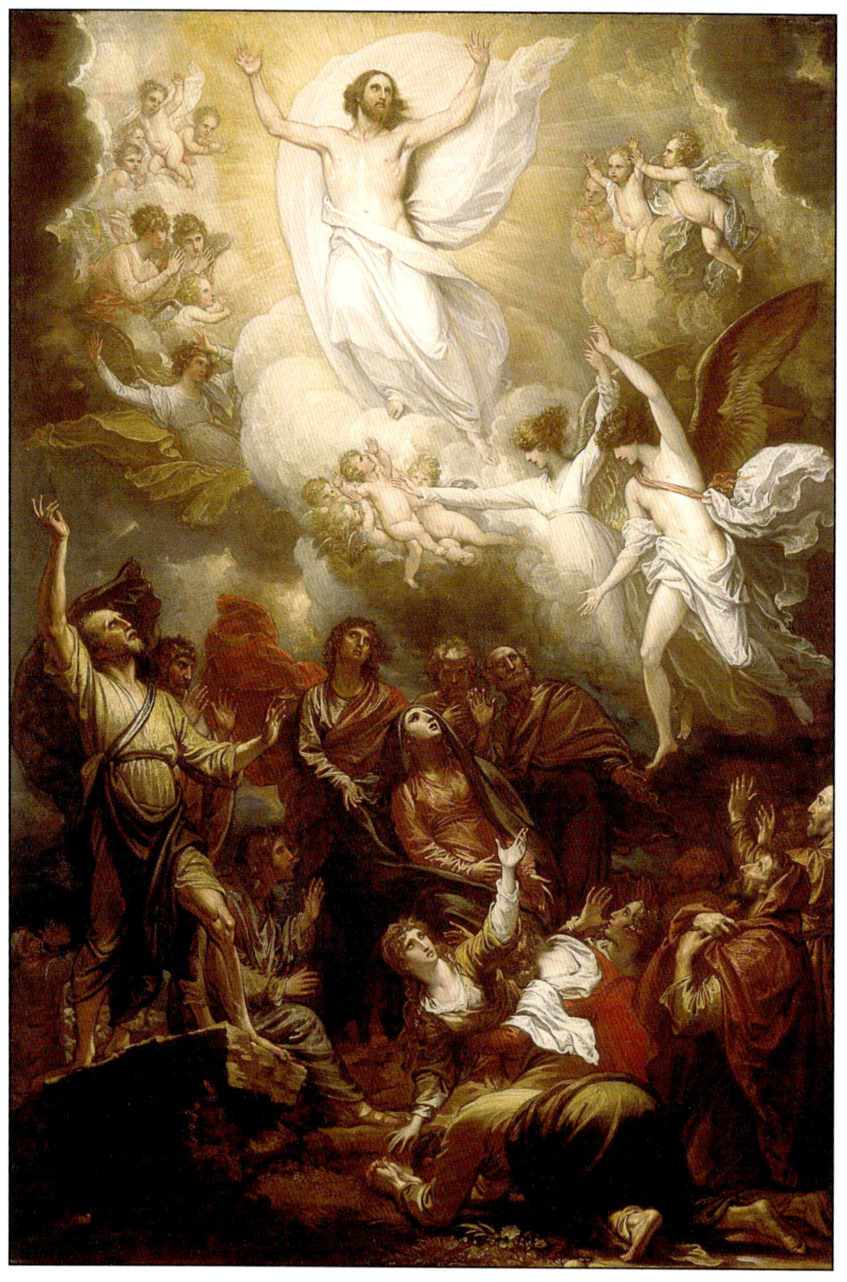

6
The Ascension

The Ascension of the Lord marks the conclusion of the Paschal Mystery. This great solemnity pulls our minds and our hearts upward as we long for full union with Jesus in glory. Still, we are reminded by the biblical record of this event, and by the sacred art that depicts it, that Christians believe there is a period of time during which we live in both worlds — both the temporal and the eternal. We are to keep to our earthly task until we "become heirs in hope of eternal life" (Titus 3:7).

The Gospels tell us very little about the Ascension. Both St. Mark and St. Luke offer readers only a few sentences, and in each, only one sentence is about Jesus' Ascension; the other sentences are about the Church's actions immediately following. The Gospels of St. Matthew and St. John do not even mention the Ascension! The Acts of the Apostles, which was also written by St. Luke, tells us the most about this astonishing event (see Acts 1:6–12).

Benjamin West was an American artist and one of the primary founders of the British Royal Academy of Art. He painted *The Ascension* in 1801, clearly relying on the account from the Acts of Apostles.[16] His masterpiece captures the sheer majesty of Jesus returning to Heaven, as well as the wonder and awe that caused the apostles and the earliest Church to worship Him and proclaim the Good News.

The focal point of this painting is the Ascended Christ. Here we call to mind St. Luke's description in his Gospel: "Then he led them [out] as far as Bethany, raised his hands, and blessed them. As he blessed them he parted from them and was taken up to heaven" (Luke 24:50–51). In this moment, the Divine Son, the Second Person of the Trinity, is returning to His original dwelling place "at the right hand of God" (Mark 16:19). The artist depicted this reality by painting Jesus wrapped in a burst of light that seems to emanate from His divine self.

Jesus raises His hands in an act that proclaims His triumphant glory and blesses those who are near Him. Here again, we can reflect on Jesus' divinity. Do I meditate on Jesus' divinity, His providence and power? Do I realize that He took on my human nature so that I might become a partaker of the divine nature (see 2 Pet. 1:4)? Do I proclaim Jesus as triumphant victor? Do I seek to be in proximity to the great Victor to receive the blessing He desires to bestow?

We also notice that the Lord's raised hands bear the scars from when they were pierced by nails. In his book *Life of Christ*, Ven. Fulton Sheen wrote about these pierced hands at the Ascension:

[16] *The Ascension*, by Benjamin West, is on display at the Denver Art Museum.

> His sacrifice being completed, as He was about to ascend to His Heavenly throne, He raised His hands bearing the imprint of nails.... The hands were raised first to heaven and then pulled downward to earth as if to draw down its blessings on men. Pierced hands best distribute benediction.[17]

Am I able to recall frequently that Jesus' Paschal Mystery, the "wounds [by which] we were healed" (Isa. 53:5), is the ultimate source of every grace and blessing that we have ever received, or will ever receive?

As we continue to meditate on this painting, we should also spend some time to reflect on the cloud on which Jesus ascends to Heaven. The Acts of the Apostles tells us that "a cloud took him from their sight" after the Lord had finished teaching (Acts 1:9). This detail causes us to remember that throughout salvation history, a cloud has always signified God's sacred presence, from the desert wanderings after the Exodus to the Transfiguration on Mount Tabor (see Exod. 13:21; Matt. 17:5). Do I acknowledge God as the guiding factor of both human history and my own history?

Not quite within the cloud, but very close, are the "two men dressed in white garments" mentioned by St. Luke (Acts. 1:10). These are angels, God's messengers, just like those mentioned in St. Luke's account of the Resurrection (see Luke 24:4–8). As we gaze on these two figures, their words to the Apostles reverberate in our minds: "Men of Galilee, why are you standing there looking at the sky?" (Acts 1:11). With this question,

[17] Sheen, *Life of Christ*, 646.

these men imply that the apostles should be looking also to the realities of earth. How has the message of the Lord come to me and how have I responded? Have I realized that the work of the Kingdom is the necessary and immediate response to the Paschal Mystery? Am I able to find a healthy balance between gazing on the glory of the Lord in prayer and meditation and engaging in works of mercy and evangelization?

Below the cloud and the angels, we notice that the lower part of the painting is quite a bit darker. This might be the artist's method of depicting the human need for divine revelation. As powerful and wonderful as human reason is, it is finite and limited. Without the aid of grace, all of us would be severely shrouded in darkness. Even the Blessed Mother, at the center of the crowd, needs grace to fully enlighten her human capacities. Do I tend to think that my own capacity for reason is sufficient for the work that I do? Do I recognize my own need for God's revelation to enlighten me?

There are eleven apostles present along with other disciples who witnessed this event. Clearly, this is the very nascent Church. Most of the figures gaze toward the Ascended Christ. Without a doubt, this seems to be an appropriate posture. But these eleven were not called to continually gaze upward. They were called to make a pilgrimage through this world, proclaiming a message that would be informed by a heavenward gaze. This is why St. Mark tells us, "They went forth and preached everywhere, while the Lord worked with them and confirmed the word through accompanying signs" (Mark 16:20). Is my whole life informed by my heavenward gaze? Is attaining Heaven my first priority? Do I seek to share the fruits of my heavenward gaze, hoping to incite a similar gaze from others? Do I share the mystery of salvation in hopes that others may also gain Heaven?

At the very bottom of the painting, one apostle falls prostrate in worship, reminding us of the words of St. Luke's Gospel (see Luke 24:52). The sheer power and glory of Our Blessed Lord lead a person to acknowledge his own lack of power and worth. The great paradox is that such an understanding becomes the most effective place from which to evangelize. When we worship God in humility, we proclaim the glory and greatness of the God-Man. Do I prostrate myself in worship before God, physically as much as spiritually?

In these days of awaiting the Promise of the Father to be "clothed with power from on high" (Luke 24:49), we all will do well to meditate on Benjamin West's memorable painting. It can remind us of God's transcendent glory as well as the mission that we have been given in this world. This piece of art, along with this solemnity, is a fantastic reminder of both dimensions of the Christian life—this world and the world to come.

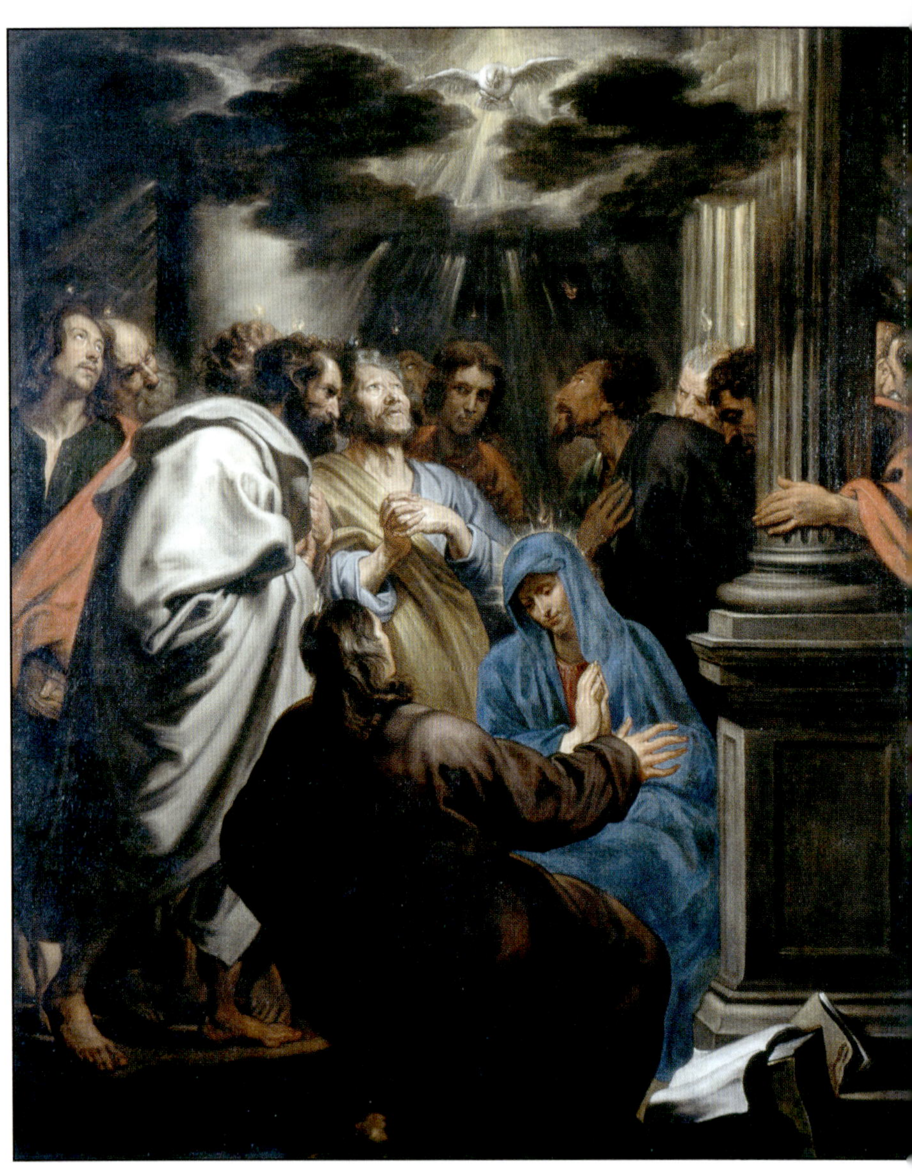

7
Outpouring of the Holy Ghost

The great solemnity of Pentecost marks the culmination of the Easter season. It is the celebration of the full harvest of God's glory and makes available to us the panoply of graces that God intends to bestow on redeemed humanity. It is also the proverbial "birthday of the Church," the moment when the new Body of Christ is brought into the world for its specific, divine purpose. It is a powerful reality, and we should hope that more and more Christians appreciate and celebrate it.

Anthony van Dyck, a Flemish artist of the Baroque period, has given us an inspiring window into the mystery and power of the Pentecost event. His painting *Outpouring of the Holy Ghost*, completed in 1620, helps us to understand the reality of this moment and the infant Church more fully. Those who gaze upon and ponder the details of this piece of art find plenty of inspiration for the Christian life.

The viewer's attention is drawn first to the top third of the image. There, we notice a dark cloud hovering over these followers of Jesus as they devote themselves to prayer in the Upper Room (Acts 1:13–14). This cloud could carry a twofold symbolic meaning. First, as we have already discussed in this book, a cloud is significant of God's presence as He guides His people. Yet a cloud also causes darkness, a shroud of unknowing and uncertainty and even fear. Perhaps the disciples were anxious because they were uncertain of what was in store, even as they hoped for the promised Advocate (see Acts 1:4–5). What has caused me to feel uncertain and fearful? Despite my uncertainty and fear, have I been able to see and know God's presence with me in any situation?

Breaking through the dark cloud is a dove, one of the most common symbols of the Holy Spirit. Looking a bit more closely, the viewer notices that this dove is coming forth from a burst of light in the shape of a triangle, both of which signify the Trinitarian God. Beyond these details, we notice that the bottom portion of the illuminated triangle is not exact and rigid. Instead, the light diffuses downward and outward, separating into rays that point toward each of those gathered in the room. Reflect on the ways that God has pierced through the dark clouds that hang over our lives and how He has poured out His very life on us. Am I able to see that the Lord does this not only for the apostles, but in every age?

The rays of light have tongues of fire at their ends. Fire, of course, is another sign of the Holy Spirit, who has come to rest on the individuals gathered here. At the center of the group is the Blessed Mother, Mary, clad in her traditional blue garment. The ray of light that touches her forms a halo of holiness around her head. One apostle, in the foreground, seems to be falling backward, as though he has been knocked over by a powerful rush of wind. These details cause us to understand a bit more fully the awesome power of this moment. Have I realized that I have also participated, substantially, in this powerful event by virtue of my own Baptism and Confirmation? Reflecting on my Baptism and Confirmation, have I understood them as the source of something new and amazing?

As we look at the group gathered, we notice that the fourteen people are all of different ages and of different ethnic origins. At the far-right edge of the painting, the face of one of the figures is covered. Since there are twelve other men painted, we surmise that this man is not meant to depict one of the apostles. This subtle detail might be intended to cause each viewer to think of his or her own presence in this group. We realize that the Church is universal: She is made up of all types of persons who seek the Lord, and She is on mission to bring all people under Her mantle. Do I realize that I am an essential part of the Church, especially by my Baptism and Confirmation? Do I realize that the mission and objective of the Church are incomplete without me serving in my God-given role?

The face of that fourteenth disciple is hidden by one of two pillars. These columns clearly point us to the Church Herself. One apostle wraps his arm around the pillar and clings to it. This might cause the viewer to ask: Do I cling to the Church, the "pillar and foundation of truth" (1 Tim. 3:15)? Do I cling to Her as I cling to Jesus, even in overwhelming moments or difficulties?

Two books are depicted at the base of the closest column, in the bottom-right corner of the painting. These are probably meant to depict the Old Testament books by which Mary and the apostles "devoted themselves . . . to prayer" in the days leading up to this event (Acts 1:14). One book, still on a stand, seems to have been vacated in a hurry, while the other has been strewn on the floor. This small detail should cause us to ponder the connection between Pentecost, as well as Christianity as a whole, and the prayer and worship of the Old Covenant, which has not been discarded but has been fulfilled and perfected. God's Chosen People, the New Israel, is able to worship and work "in Spirit and truth" as Jesus promised in Samaria (John 4:23–24), especially by the power bestowed to us at Pentecost. Do I venerate the revelation of the Old Testament, allowing it to open up a deeper understanding of the fullness of God's plan found in Jesus and the Church?

Each of us who ponders Van Dyck's painting is mystically brought into the mysterious and powerful moment of Pentecost. By reflecting on its themes and the questions it opens up, each of us can find assistance and inspiration for becoming better disciples in the Christian mission. Finally, we walk away from viewing this painting knowing that we have been chosen by God and sent into the world to accomplish His purposes. Let's pray that we spend the remainder of the liturgical year, and every year, accomplishing that mission.

PART V

The Art of Jesus' Public Ministry

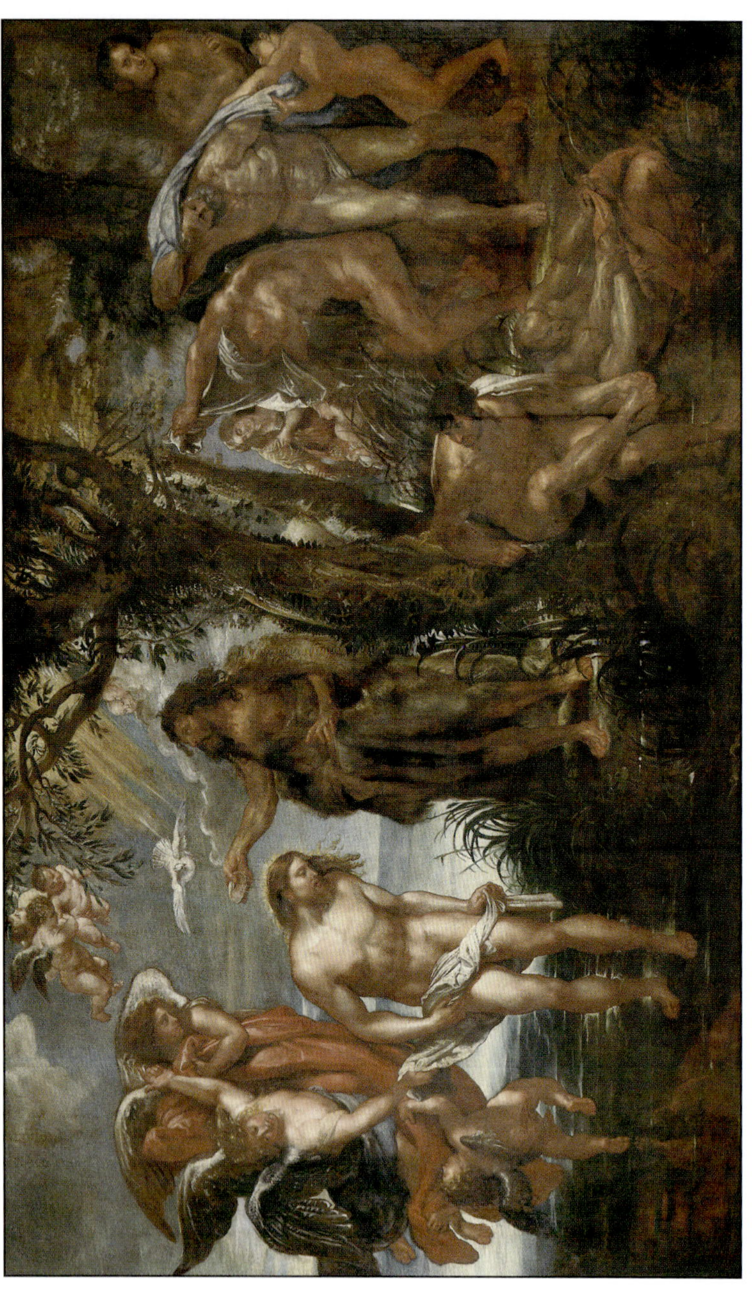

I

The Baptism of Christ

St. Matthew's Gospel tells us that Jesus' public ministry was a period during which the Messiah went about Judea and Samaria and the surrounding region "teaching in their synagogues, proclaiming the gospel of the kingdom, and curing every disease and illness among the people" (Matt. 4:23). This ministry, which was "to proclaim liberty to captives and recovery of sight to the blind, [and] to let the oppressed go free" (Luke 4:18), was inaugurated by His Baptism in the Jordan River. Each Gospel recounts the event's occurrence, revealing its importance for what would come after.

Many intriguing renditions of this biblical event have been painted throughout Christian history. Yet one of the most memorable versions was completed in 1605 by Dutch artist Peter Paul Rubens, titled *The Baptism of Christ*. As we reflect on this biblical event, specifically through this painting, we are able to recognize and reflect deeply on the most important contours and themes of Jesus' whole ministry.

In the center of the painting stands the gruff, bearded John the Baptist, with his arm outstretched to pour water over Jesus' head. Covering John's body is the camel-hair garment referenced in Matthew's Gospel. He stands next to a tree, which could have multiple layers of meaning. It might represent the Tree of Knowledge of Good and Evil from the Garden of Eden, which was the source of the Original Sin, the effects of which Jesus was sent to overcome and undo. It might also reference John's warning to the Pharisees and Sadducees: "Every tree that does not bear good fruit will be cut down and thrown into the fire" (Matt. 3:10). No matter the particular meaning, this tree provides a dividing point in the two halves of the painting.

On the same side of the painting as the Baptist, Jesus stands in the Jordan River, barely wearing a white garment. Jesus is more radiant than any other figure in the painting, which causes viewers to ponder what might be the greatest lesson from this piece of art. We are reminded of the words of St. John in his first letter: "God is light, and in him there is no darkness at all" (1 John 1:5). This bit of divine revelation ought to tell us, first, that the light and radiance of Jesus Christ surpass anything else that we can know in life. Then, we might begin to ask how we can participate in the divine light that Jesus brings—how we can push back the darkness that tries to envelop our lives.

Directly above Jesus' head and John's baptizing hand is a dove, the symbol of the Holy Spirit that was recorded by each of the four Gospel authors. This dove flies down from the end of rays of light that pour forth from the opened heavens. At this moment in the biblical text, we hear that "a voice came from heaven," clearly the voice of the Heavenly Father, and made a crucial proclamation: "You are my beloved Son; with you I am well pleased" (Luke 3:22). This statement must be foundational in the life and spirituality of every disciple and seeker. All of us are God's beloved children, particularly those of us who have received the Sacrament of Baptism. By this very fact, God is pleased with us. We might sin, we may even stray far from divine life in the Church, but God is infinitely pleased that each baptized person has been brought into the potential life-giving relationship through this foundational sacrament.

Around Jesus and above St. John are a host of angels. As the viewer gazes at this part of the scene, she is quickly reminded of the "multitude of the heavenly host … praising God" at the great Nativity of the Lord (Luke 2:13). The angels closest to Jesus seem to be helping Him shed the white garment that He wore before His Baptism, and they seem ready to place on Him the red garment of sacrifice. Of course, we know that Our Blessed Lord wore both of these garments perfectly. How do I wear these two garments of Christianity in my own life? How do I connect frequently to the graces and call of my Baptism? How have I recognized sacrifice as part of answering my baptismal call?

Finally, behind the Baptist on the other side of the tree, we see a number of shadowy figures, including some that seem almost demonic. Most of them are unclothed and seem to be drying off after their own baptisms. Only one of the figures looks at Jesus, while the others continue about their basic tasks of getting dressed or fixing their hair. This detail offers each viewer the opportunity to ask a probing question: As a baptized Christian, am I focused on Jesus, or do I merely go about my business, allowing myself to be distracted from our Lord? Do I continue to connect with Jesus through the graces that He has offered to me in Baptism?

The scene that Rubens painted invites us to consider the light that Jesus carried into the world and to ask where we stand in relation to Jesus' ministry and how we are receiving or rejecting the light that the Lord brings. Ultimately, it causes each of us to recognize whether, and to what degree, we are becoming the children that the Heavenly Father wants us to become — to assess whether we are really pleasing God by our daily lives.

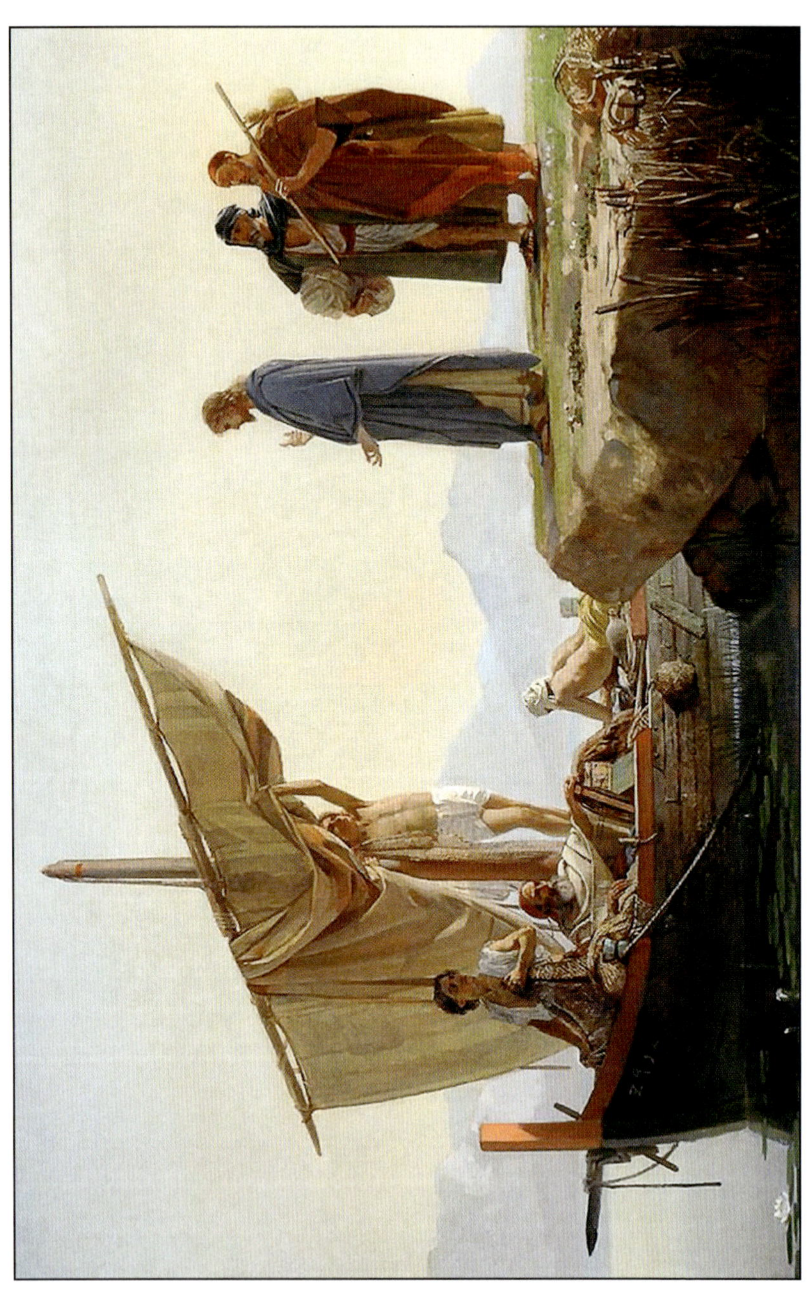

2

Christ Calling the Apostles James and John

THE GOSPELS OF Sts. Matthew, Mark, and Luke tell us that very soon after His Baptism, Jesus called His first disciples by the Sea of Galilee. The four names specifically provided to readers in those accounts are Andrew, Simon, James, and John. These are the first four men to become apostles, the leaders of the New Israel that Jesus intended to establish.

One of the best artistic depictions of Jesus inviting others to minister with Him is *Christ Calling the Apostles James and John*, by Edward Armitage, from 1869. This painting seems to rely on St. Mark's Gospel account, as it is the only one that mentions the hired servants in Zebedee's boat (see Mark 1:19–20), yet it also uses details from all the Gospel accounts. These details identify the mission that Jesus intended to accomplish in the world and through the Church for all future ages.

At the very outset, the viewer notices the painting's setting. Armitage depicts a rocky shoreline and mountainous terrain in the background. He presents us with a keen sense of the place where Jesus first encountered and invited these four men so that we may enter more fully into the biblical narrative (see Mark 1:16–20).

After processing the setting, the viewer's eyes are quickly drawn to Jesus, who is cloaked in blue. We have identified in other essays that this color signifies His divinity. Yet we notice that He is walking among men, engaging in ordinary human actions. This ought to bring us to a deeper appreciation of the teaching provided by St. John in the theological prologue to his Gospel account: "And the Word became flesh and made his dwelling among us, and we saw his glory, the glory as of the Father's only Son, full of grace and truth" (John 1:14). Quite simply, Jesus reveals the Heavenly Father to us, even and especially through His ordinary actions in this world.

Near the center of the canvas, we notice Jesus' hands. One hand is extended and opened toward those who hear the proposal, "Follow me" (Mark 1:17, ESV). The other hand points upward, as if to the Heavenly Father, who longs for communion with us through Jesus, His Son. By these gestures, the Lord presents His whole proposition to any potential disciple. Answering this invitation, though it may be confusing and challenging, places one on a spiritual trajectory to a full relationship with God. Do I recognize that communion with Jesus, and the other two Persons of the Trinity, involves both upward and outward focus? Do I tend to focus more on my spiritual relationship with God, or on the good works that make the Gospel incarnate? What needs to happen for me to balance these two halves of the same reality?

Behind Jesus are two men carrying some belongings. These are clearly Simon and Andrew, who made the decision to follow

Jesus just before the moment captured here. What do they carry? We know they left much behind, including their boat and nets, along with at least some family at home, since in both Mark's and Luke's Gospels, Jesus cures Simon's mother-in-law (Mark 1:29–31; Luke 4:38–39). One of the men wields a walking stick, probably significant of all the walking these men would do around the region with Jesus. Every one of us is offered the same invitation these men received. Am I ready and willing to travel the unknown journey with the Lord? If so, what do I absolutely need for the journey, and what am I willing to leave behind?

The focal point of this scene seems to be the four men whom Jesus faces as He speaks to them and extends His invitation. The first figure the viewer may notice is the one closest to Jesus. He has his back turned to the Messiah and engages in some unknown task. It is always significant in a piece of art when one character is orientated away from the painting's focal point. In this case, the artist probably wants to indicate that there are always individuals who ignore Jesus' invitation and message for the sake of some menial task of lesser gravity. This detail might cause the viewer to meditate briefly on the capital sin of sloth, which is refusal to engage in one's heavenly task or mission: Have I refused to take up, with courage and diligence, the task that Jesus has placed before me? Or have I allowed myself to make other things, such as mundane work or chores, a higher priority than a life-giving relationship with Jesus?

Two of the men in the boat are seated and mending fishing nets. These two, probably James and Zebedee, bear perplexed, even skeptical or wary, looks on their faces. We know from the biblical text that James left his father to answer Jesus' call. As we look at these two figures, we ought to question ourselves: Have I ever been skeptical or wary of Jesus' invitation? Why? Have I been willing to leave behind livelihood and even family for the sake of a deeper relationship and the surprises it may offer? What has caused me to remain behind?

The youngest sailor at the center of the boat, probably John, lifts the boat's sail as if to see and hear Jesus more clearly. This detail fosters an interesting consideration. Just as he lifts the sail in the painting, John also used the words, stories, and images of his Gospel to invite readers to lift the veil of Jesus' humanity and see more deeply into the Lord's divinity. Do I see that God invites me to a deeper understanding of Trinitarian life through the Person of Jesus? Have I ever really, even anxiously, removed obstacles to seeing and hearing Jesus more clearly? Have I read and prayed with the Bible? Have I considered Sacred Scripture for what it really is, an opportunity to see beyond the veil of this world into divine things?

The proximity of the two parts of the scene is also worth consideration. Four characters occupy the boat that floats on the water. Jesus, Simon, and Andrew are elevated on a plateau of sorts, and so James and John will need to exert some great effort in order to leave their father's boat and join the other three. This effort should not be construed as some sort of "righteousness by works." Rather, it simply provides a visual depiction of the gravity, the challenge, of deciding to follow Jesus. It is never easy, nor will it ever be, to follow Christ, but Christian disciples must renew our commitment to Him and strive to be like Him every day. The impassable chasms and arduous realities of Christian discipleship become passable and more facile when we let the Lord's grace lead the way and then take the simple steps to answer His call.

This simple scene painted by Armitage is so beneficial because it allows us to ponder many important aspects of the Christian life: the call from Jesus, the required decision from each person, the importance of a cohesive vision and effort in a community, and the terminus of a disciple's life and efforts. It also points toward the mysterious and miraculous public ministry of Jesus. Let us pray that as we prayerfully sit with this image and its details, we are intrigued enough to make the same decision as these first apostles and to walk their same path.

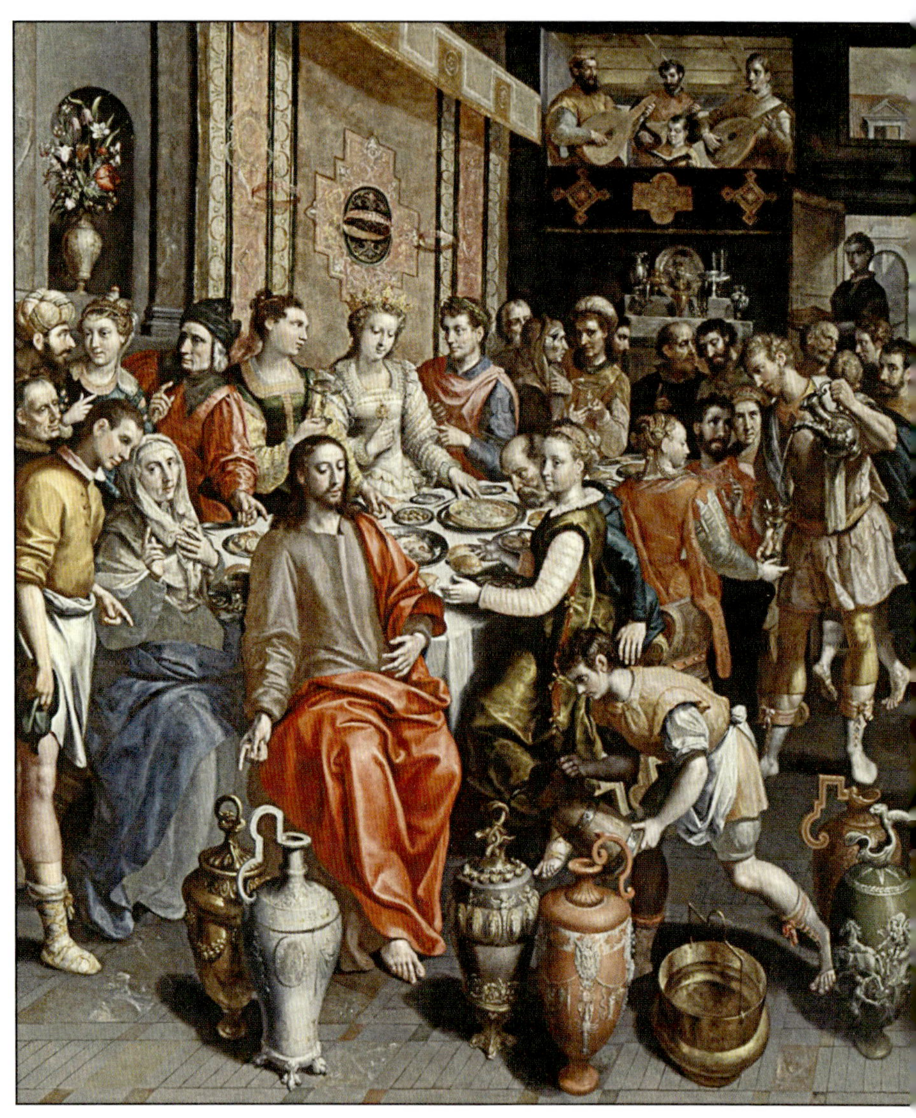

3

The Marriage at Cana

JESUS' PUBLIC MINISTRY had two crucial and related aspects: our Blessed Lord intended to bring life and light and peace to those who would believe in His name, and He intended finally to gather the full family of God together in one Body. It is no surprise, then, that Jesus performed the first miracle of His public ministry at a wedding feast, since marriage is the foundation of the family and society. At the Wedding at Cana, the Savior provided a luminous grace to all who were witness, and we can receive that same grace today, two millennia later, as we ponder this event. This first miracle invites us to turn to Jesus in faith and petition for ourselves and for others to be strengthened in our arduous journey (see CCC 514, 542, 548).

In 1597, Flemish artist Maerten de Vos painted *The Marriage at Cana*. De Vos's rendition of this biblical event connects viewers with the reality of Jesus' ministry, helping them access the light that Our Lord brings to the world and to our lives. It leaves a lasting impression of this important moment in the life of Jesus, and it has much to teach us.

Immediately, the viewer notices the disposition of the crowd in this scene. Nearly every guest at this wedding celebration is looking somewhere other than at Jesus. The people are preoccupied with their own conversations and their own lives. Of course, this would have been natural in this moment, as Jesus had been living in silence and anonymity in Nazareth for nearly His whole life. Still, the fact that the wedding guests were oblivious should elicit a question in each person who views this artwork: Am I going about my life distracted and unaware of Jesus' presence, even if He is close and is prepared to perform miracles in my life?

While all the other guests are totally engrossed in the food and festivities, there are two guests on Jesus' left who notice that Jesus is preparing to perform a miracle. One of them, an older man, stares at the Lord with intense incredulity. He seems to say, "I'll believe it, but I need to see it." The other is a young woman who is looking directly out of the scene at the viewer while pointing to Jesus with both hands. It is as if she is saying to every one of us, "You need to watch this man. This is going to be really important." This pair of wedding guests can help every viewer to ask a self-reflective question: Am I another Doubting Thomas, or am I anticipating the Lord's action in faith and hope?

Jesus Himself is the focal point of the painting. He reclines at table, covered by a red garment. The color of the garment signifies the fact that Our Blessed Lord's ministry was inaugurated to culminate in the Crucifixion at Golgotha. Ven. Fulton Sheen wrote that this wedding feast was indeed the beginning of Jesus' "hour," the threshold moment that would initiate

His pilgrimage to the Cross.[18] As we ponder the Wedding Feast at Cana, we ought to remember that relationship with Jesus requires our own *via crucis*, our own Way of the Cross (see Matt. 16:24; Mark 8:34; Luke 9:23). But we also must remember that Jesus walks that Way of the Cross with us.

Next to Jesus is His Blessed Mother, Mary, cloaked in the blue of divinity as usual. She holds a finger in the air while she talks to one of the stewards of the celebration. This is clearly the moment when she speaks her final recorded words in Scripture: "Do whatever he tells you" (John 2:5). So much of the Christian life flows from this concept of obedience to Jesus. Each and every disciple must take frequent opportunities to examine whether or not he is fully obedient to the Lord or if he harbors personal tendencies to distrust and pride.

The steward to whom Mary speaks is also worth a sustained glance. As he listens to this unknown woman, the look on his face seems to say, "Okay, I'm going to do what he tells me. I'm not sure what is going to happen, but I'm really looking forward to seeing something special here." He also points toward the large carafes of wine, to which Jesus also points. The fact that both fingers point to the same location illustrates an important trend of the spiritual life. We should want to point in the same direction, to the same place, as Jesus. More than that, we should be fed, sustained, and lifted up by seeing the miraculous works that Our Lord does in the world, even things that might be called "natural" by so many others. Everyday miracles have the potential to keep any of us from becoming Doubting Thomases.

[18] Sheen, *Life of Christ*, 88–91.

Finally, there is a Trinitarian motif in this painting. Above the bride and groom, three lute players, along with a young vocalist, provide music for the celebration. The three older men could very well be symbolic of the Trinity. This detail can help remind viewers of the fact that the Holy Trinity sings joyfully over every holy marriage that is entered into humbly and earnestly. Like the bride, groom, wedding guests, Mary, and Jesus, we all can rejoice in God's favor upon marriage.

For all these reasons, De Vos's painting is unique and special. It invites viewers to learn or recall important realities about theology and patterns of the Christian life, helps bring basic spiritual questions into our minds and hearts, and allows us to access more of the light by which Jesus wants to illuminate our lives. The light we receive by pondering Jesus, His public ministry, and His Passion and Resurrection should incite us to continue to share His grace with those around us.

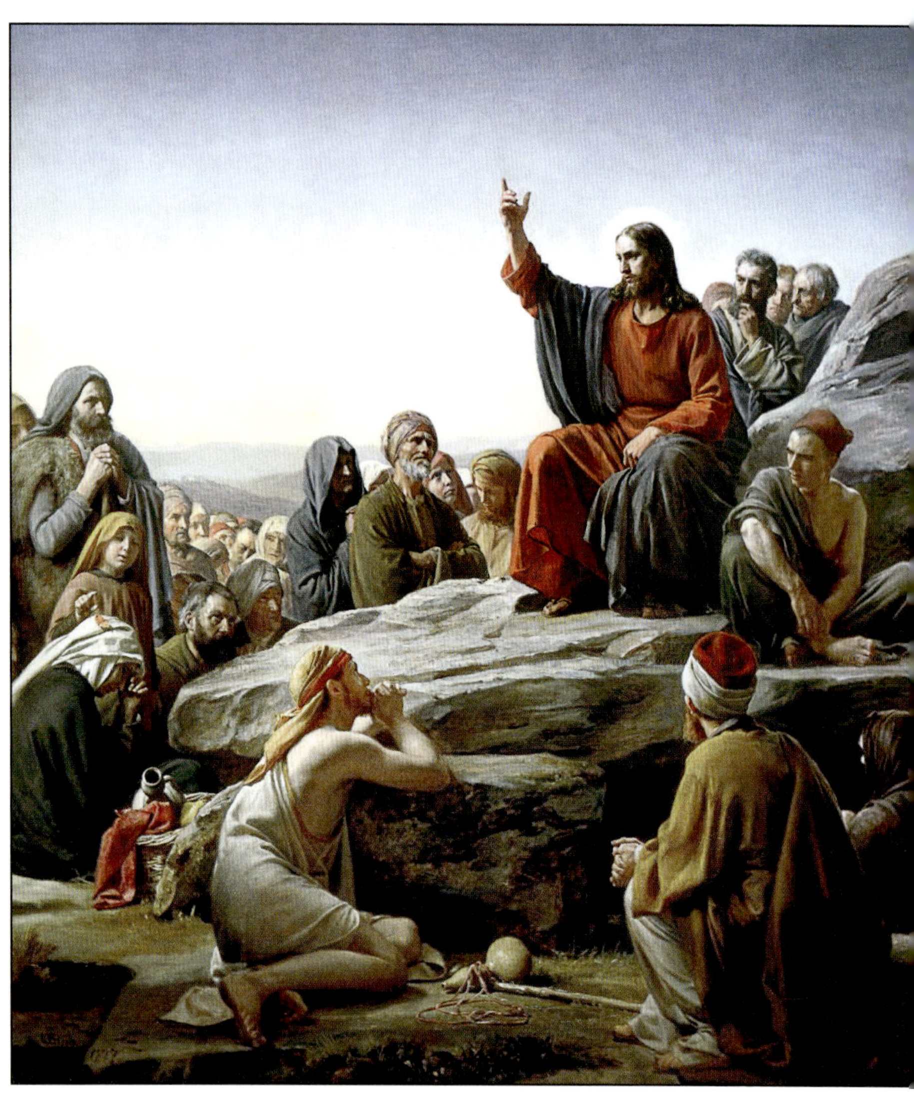

4

Sermon on the Mount

THROUGHOUT HIS PUBLIC ministry, Jesus proclaimed that the Kingdom of God was near, even present among the people at that very moment. During those years, Jesus taught in parables and gave instruction on how to live, cured physical ailments and deformities, and healed spiritual infirmities by casting out demons and forgiving sins.

The myriad layers of Jesus' proclamation of the Kingdom necessitate reflection on multiple pieces of art, each of which identifies a particular element of the proclamation. We will start our reflection with the event by which Jesus initiated His proclamation, the Sermon on the Mount. Carl Heinrich Bloch, a renowned Danish artist of the nineteenth century, painted his rendition of the *Sermon on the Mount* near the end of his noteworthy career in 1877, and it remains one of the most identifiable and memorable pieces in Christian art. The elements of this painting allow us to prepare for the astonishing miracles that Jesus would perform and to bask more fully in the light that He brought to the world.

Jesus Christ Himself is the visual center of the painting. The viewer's eyes immediately notice that He is dressed in red, which can symbolize passion, love, and fire and also probably indicates the *via crucis*, the road to Jesus' sacrificial death that began as soon as He started teaching and performing miracles. This detail also reminds viewers that discipleship is a personal commitment that requires passion, love, fire (a sign of the Holy Spirit), and a *via crucis* of our own (see Luke 9:23).

We also notice that our Lord's right hand is raised, pointing to Heaven. This reminds us that every word and action of Our Blessed Lord's proclamation was meant to point us toward Our Heavenly Father and to bring us fully into relationship with Him. Each of us must ask probing questions about our response to this opportunity. Have I grown closer to the Heavenly Father recently? Have my desires and actions changed to make that happen? If not, what's preventing me?

After taking in the details about Jesus and His posture, we notice other figures nearby. First, at Jesus' right, we see an older man wearing a look of disdain on his face. Perhaps the artist intended him to represent the Pharisaical establishment that would be so roiled by Jesus' radical and paradoxical teachings of humility, mercy, and charity. Perhaps the look on this man's face causes each of us to think about ways that we have rejected the full truth of revelation, choosing only the parts that suit our preferences. Have I fallen prey to the leaven of the Pharisees by focusing too much on the letter of the law at the expense of mercy or charity? Have I focused too much on maintaining my own image, influence, or power to the detriment of right relationship with God and others?

Two other figures in the painting warrant extended reflection. A bearded man stands behind Jesus, quizzically pondering what the Teacher has to say. It appears that this man isn't quite sure what to make of the paradoxical message of the Beatitudes. On Jesus' left side is a younger man. While his back is turned to the Messiah, his head is turned toward Jesus, and the look on his face implies that he is deeply intrigued and astonished by what he hears. Both of these men show dispositions that are common in every age. Do we really hear Jesus saying what we think we hear? Do we have trouble making sense of His amazing and perplexing words? Do we turn our backs to Jesus but still strain our necks in an attempt to look like we're listening?

At Jesus' feet are two men whose hands are folded in prayer. One, whose back is completely to the viewer, looks as though he might be from a higher social class. The other is clearly a poor shepherd who has cast aside the tools of his trade. These figures reveal to us at least two important truths. First, the proclamation of Jesus is for any person of any social class. When we become part of the Chosen People of God, we all stand side-by-side as equals, regardless of status or wealth. Second, when Jesus begins to speak His truth to us, we must become willing to cast aside even the few comforts and certainties we may have. We should ask ourselves: Do I live by these principles in my own journey with Jesus?

To the left of the shepherd is a basket of household goods, including a water jug and some laundry garments. The basket sits beside a downcast woman who is clearly overwhelmed with grief, anxiety, and stress. This woman represents all those in the Gospel and in our own age who have been beaten down by life, those to whom Jesus' proclamation is spoken most specifically (see Luke 4:16–21). Each of us can identify with this woman's disposition, and we can hear Jesus speak to her emotions:

> The Spirit of the Lord is upon me, because he has anointed me to bring glad tidings to the poor. He has sent me to proclaim liberty to captives and recovery of sight to the blind, to let the oppressed go free, and to proclaim a year acceptable to the Lord. (Luke 4:18–19)

An orange butterfly rests on the woman's white head covering. This ought to signify the transformation that is available for those who will hear Jesus' words and begin to practice them daily. The Sermon on the Mount was the first verbal proclamation of the impending and already-present Kingdom (see Luke 17:21), the first great ray of light from the Source of All Light that would only grow as Jesus traveled and taught and healed. All of us who view this painting ought to be inspired by the potential resurrection to new life that is provided by the grace of God and made present in the Incarnate Word.

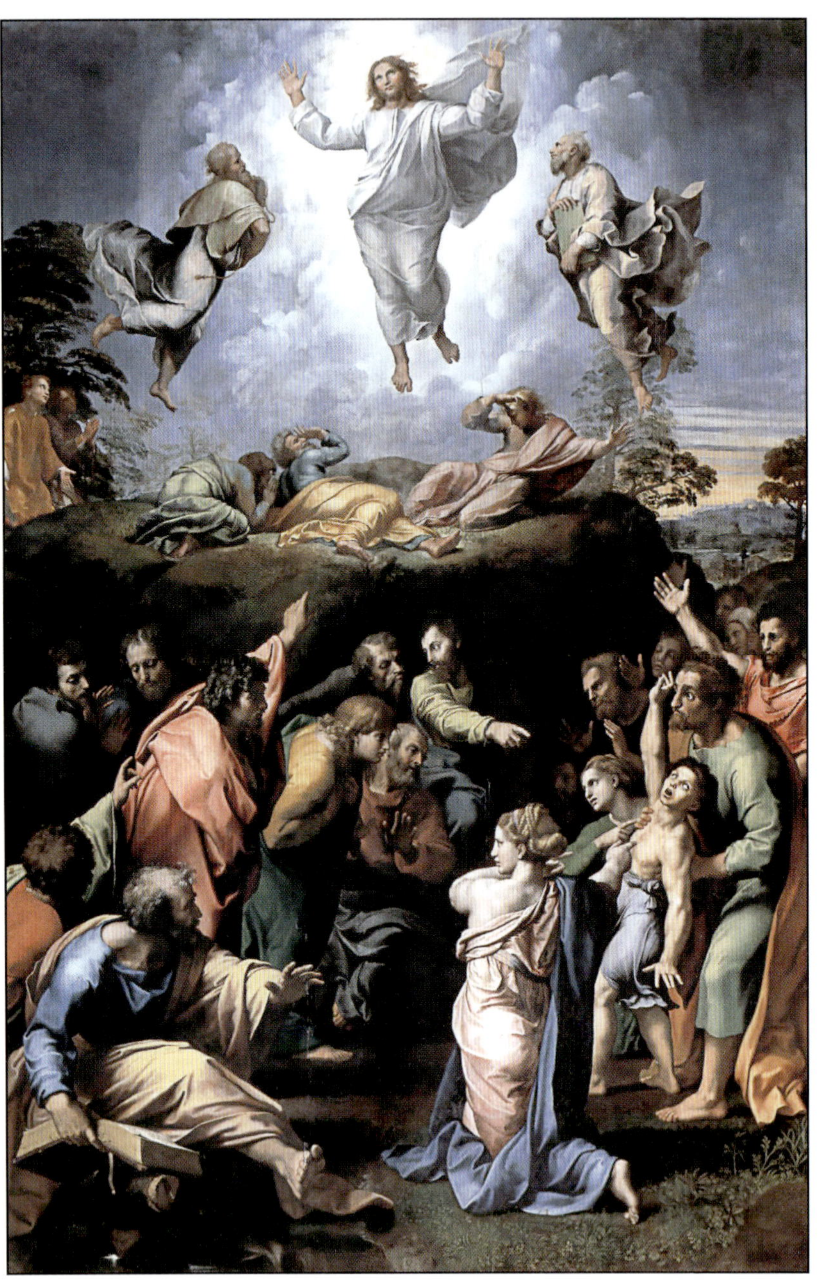

5
The Transfiguration

THE TRANSFIGURATION OF Jesus on Mount Tabor is a climactic point in Jesus' public ministry. Pope St. John Paul II, in his apostolic letter on the Rosary, calls it the "mystery of light *par excellence*." The purpose of this important event was to prepare the apostles "to experience with him the agony of the Passion, so as to come with him to the joy of the Resurrection and a life transfigured by the Holy Spirit."[19] The mystery of the Transfiguration therefore draws a profound connection between Jesus' Sermon on the Mount, His miracles and healings, and His sacrificial death on Mount Calvary.

Raffaelo Sanzio, better known to posterity as Raphael, was one of the artistic masters of the Italian Renaissance. In 1516, at the age of thirty-three, he was commissioned to paint *The Transfiguration* as an altarpiece for the Narbonne Cathedral in France. He completed it in 1520, just before his death at the age of thirty-seven. Many historians and art commentators,

[19] Pope St. John Paul II, apostolic letter *Rosarium Virginis Mariae* (October 16, 2002), no. 21.

as well as the artist himself, consider this final painting to be Raphael's *magnum opus*. This altarpiece presents two halves of a story, both of which are recorded in the seventeenth chapter of Matthew's Gospel. Raphael's masterpiece is also ripe for personal reflection, as it helps us to glean a deeper understanding of this mystical event and its connection to the healing mercy of Jesus Christ.

The top half of the altarpiece depicts the mystical event that took place atop Mount Tabor. At the top center is the focal point of the whole image, the transfigured Jesus. He is lifted up from *terra firma* and surrounded by a large cloud, which is brighter closer to its center. This cloud indicates to the viewer that Jesus is truly connected with the God who led Israel through the desert with a pillar of cloud or fire (see Exod. 13:17–22). This detail causes us to ask: Do I allow Jesus Christ, His person and His ministry, to enlighten me and reveal the fullness of God's love to me?

Another fascinating element of the top half of the altarpiece is the interconnected triangles that Raphael painted into the scene. Jesus is the apex of the first triangle, and Moses and Elijah form the sides. This first triangle therefore presents a visual depiction of the revelation that Jesus Christ is the summation of the law and the prophets of the Old Covenants.

The second triangle is formed by Jesus' two raised hands and right foot. The shape narrows as it moves downward, coming near the mountain and the three apostles. This triangle is a visual representation of the important theological point that Jesus, in the Incarnation, assumed a human nature. This downward triangle puts a shape to St. Paul's teaching about

Jesus' ultimate act of humility: Although Jesus existed in "the form of God," He "emptied himself" and was "born in the likeness of men. And being found in human form, he humbled himself" (Phil. 2:6–8, ESV).

The second Person of the Trinity became human so humans, like these apostles, could have more intimate access to God. This is precisely why a voice "from the cloud" instructed Peter, James, and John to "listen to him" (Matt. 17:5). Listening to the teachings of Jesus and imitating the example of His actions will draw us more deeply, "upward," into the divine life. Every disciple has to ask: How do I heed the teaching of Jesus? How am I called to empty myself in imitation of His humility?

Below the Messiah and the prophets are the three apostles who were led "up a high mountain by themselves" (Matt. 17:1). These figures lie prostrate, shielding their faces. Noting the apostles' postures should cause the viewer to ask: Am I astonished by the powerful revelation of Jesus Christ? Do I have trouble assimilating that revelation into my body, mind, and spirit?

The most noticeable and interesting details about the apostles are the colors that they wear. The artist intended the colors to reveal the connection that each man has to one of the theological virtues. St. Peter wears blue for his incredible statements of faith, such as, "You are the Messiah, the Son of the living God" (Matt. 16:16). St. James, on the left, wears green because he wrote about the hope and joy that come from living one's faith through daily effort. St. John, on the right, wears red for charity, which is the primary theme of his Gospel account and New Testament letters. Witnessing the Transfiguration increased the theological virtues in these men, making them ready to share in Jesus' Passion. How am I growing in faith, hope, and charity? How am I being prepared to walk my own *via crucis*?

The bottom half of the altarpiece presents the episode that immediately followed Jesus' Transfiguration. Upon descending Mount Tabor, the Messiah was approached by a father who asked for a miraculous healing of his demon-possessed son. This father, dressed in green, holds his son upright. This man had brought his son to the other nine apostles while Jesus and the three apostles were atop the mountain, but "they could not cure him" (Matt. 17:16). This part of the scene causes the viewer to ask: Do I have a habit of bringing those in need into Jesus' merciful, healing presence? If I am unable to do this physically, do I make it a reality through intercessory prayer?

On the left-hand side of the lower half are nine apostles. Here, Raphael gives expression to their confusion about their inability to heal. Most of these figures focus their attention on the demoniac boy, and several of them appear to be arguing among themselves. Only two of the apostles turn their attention and point toward Jesus. This portion of the scene allows each of us to ponder our own confusion, insecurity, and lack of efficacy in our works. Have I taken time to meditate on Jesus' answer to the apostles that they could not heal him because of their lack of faith (see Matt. 17:20)? Have I connected this message with what Jesus spoke in another Gospel passage: "Whoever remains in me and I in him will bear much fruit, because without me you can do nothing" (John 15:5)?

The figure in the bottom left of the painting draws the viewer more deeply into the anticipation of Jesus' mighty works. This is St. Matthew, identified by the book that represents the Gospel account he writes. St. Matthew gestures to the viewer as if to say, "Wait! Watch! Something amazing is happening here." This allows the viewer to examine his own life: Do I eagerly anticipate Jesus' miracles in my life? Do I trust that He can and will perform those miracles so that I can be transformed like Peter, James, John, and the other apostles, and healed like the demoniac boy?

In his final masterpiece, Raphael makes an important point about Christian discipleship. His painting of *The Transfiguration* reminds viewers that mystical experiences and ongoing works of faith and mercy were not separated in Jesus' ministry, and they cannot be separated in our lives. While we may sometimes feel hopeless and that our works and prayers are ineffective, we must remember that all can be transfigured and transformed if we focus first on Jesus and then on the works that He has given each of us to do. Then we can reflect His light and continue to do His work in the world.

PART VI

The Art of Jesus' Parables & Miracles

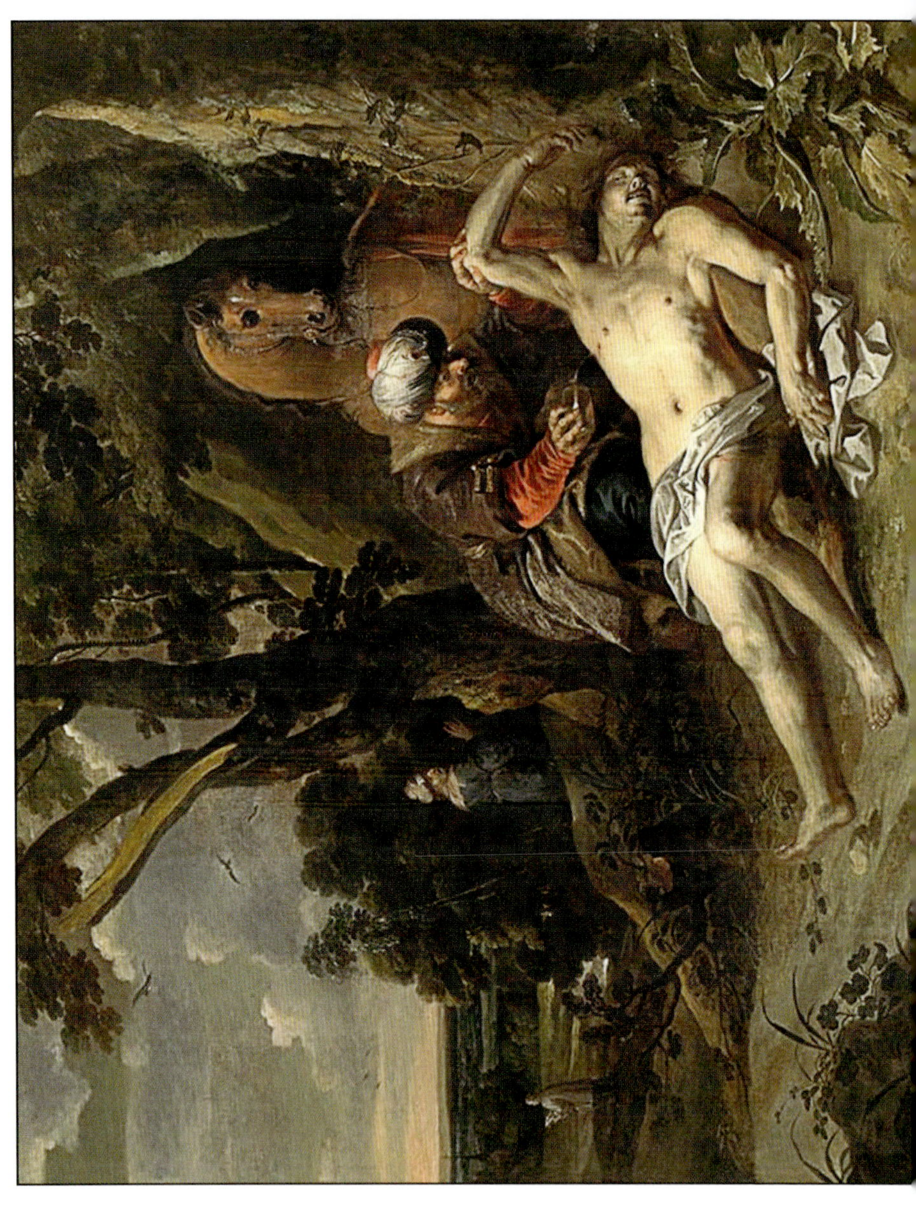

I

The Good Samaritan

After the Sermon on the Mount, which was the summation of Jesus' teachings about the moral and spiritual life, our Lord continued to give instruction on how to live through His parables. Of the many parables Jesus employed to teach about the Kingdom of God, one of the most memorable and significant is the parable of the good samaritan (see Luke 10:29–37).

Balthasar van Cortbemde, a Flemish art dealer from Antwerp, visualized this parable when he painted *The Good Samaritan* in 1647. The painting, which is the only work attributed to the artist during his career, draws viewers into the biblical scene and offers them the opportunity to ponder the position and movements of its various characters. In these moments of reflection, we can meditate on how Jesus exercised His ministry of mercy and how we can participate in and extend that ministry.

We read in Luke's Gospel, "A man was going down from Jerusalem to Jericho, and he fell among robbers, who stripped him and beat him and departed, leaving him half dead" (Luke 10:30, ESV). We see this beaten man in the foreground of the painting, covered in nothing but a dusty shred of white cloth. Upon looking at this man, the viewer might associate him with Jesus taken down from the Cross. In any case, pondering this part of the image allows the viewer to ask probing questions: What have been the patterns in my life that have left me stripped, beaten, and half-dead? Are there people who have taken advantage of me in those ways? Have I ever acted as one of the robbers, abusing others and leaving them wounded?

The viewer notices quickly that the beaten man has a wound on the right side of his torso, near his heart. This certainly could be symbolic of the way that sin, both our own and others', inflicts deep wounds on our bodies, minds, and spirits. How have I been wounded by sin, and whose sin has wounded me?

Kneeling over the wounded man is the so-called Good Samaritan. His position indicates that he "was moved with compassion" (Luke 10:33). He is depicted in attire from the Middle and Far East. This is probably meant to show the difference in culture between these two men, the difference that normally would have kept the man from lending his aid. In my own life, am I willing to receive help and healing from someone unexpected, even someone from outside of my social norms?

The Samaritan pours an elixir from a balm jar into the beaten man's wound. The biblical passage tells us that he "poured oil and wine over his wounds and bandaged them"

(Luke 10:34). Throughout salvation history, oil has always been a symbol of healing as well as a mark of ownership, and wine has always been a symbol of abundant joy. This detail can help develop in viewers a deeper devotion to the sacraments, especially the Anointing of the Sick, Baptism, Confirmation, and the Eucharist, in which the Lord marks us, sustains us, and brings us new joy.

It seems that the inn to which the Samaritan would transport the man is at the left-hand edge of the scene. We notice, though, that it is depicted with a cross atop a steeple, as a parish church. From the time of the Church Fathers, the inn in the parable has been symbolic of the Church in Her structure and ministry. Like the Samaritan, do we have trust and confidence in the innkeepers (especially the clergy) to provide effective and sustained ministry, especially spiritual healing, particularly in these recent years of scandal and secularization?

In between these two parts of the scene, we notice two other figures. The first is the priest who has passed by some time ago. We notice that he is occupied with a book, perhaps a breviary, as he walks. The other figure is the Levite who looks back over his shoulder at the Samaritan and the injured man. We know from the biblical parable that he chose to pass by the man in need, but the artist shows that he is interested in the outcome. These figures cause us to ask ourselves if there have been times in which we have ignored or avoided some distressed person for what seemed like a legitimate reason. Perhaps later we have realized in hindsight that we should have done more. In any case, this parable and this painting offer each of us an opportunity to reflect on how we can extend more of Jesus' mercy to those around us. We know from the Lord's teaching, and from the example of several figures in the Gospels, that we must always be alert and ready to respond to His direction—and that it is never too late to begin, even if we have been neglectful in the past.

The last detail that may be worthy of some reflection is the tree under which the Samaritan anoints the wounded man. This tree has a branch that is severely broken, and part of it lies on the ground. Perhaps the artist sought to make a visual commentary about the fracturing of Europe that had taken place for roughly a century. Van Cortbemde lived near the end of an extensive series of wars of religion, rooted in the Protestant Reformation, that divided and racked the central and northwestern portions of the continent. Even in our own day, when wars are largely of a different origin and kind, we can still reflect on the ways that such events have rent the human community and ask if there is any way that we can foster healing. How can we bring the mercy of Jesus to someone in need, regardless of ethnic, religious, or social boundaries?

Reading this parable and gazing at this painting allow us to gain a fuller understanding of the ways that the Sermon on the Mount is to be implemented in our lives and open a window to see the extension of Jesus' ministry of mercy. That ministry includes looking past social boundaries in solidarity. That ministry revolves around the Church and

Her sacraments. And that ministry beckons us to bring the works of mercy to a sinful world full of brokenness and need.

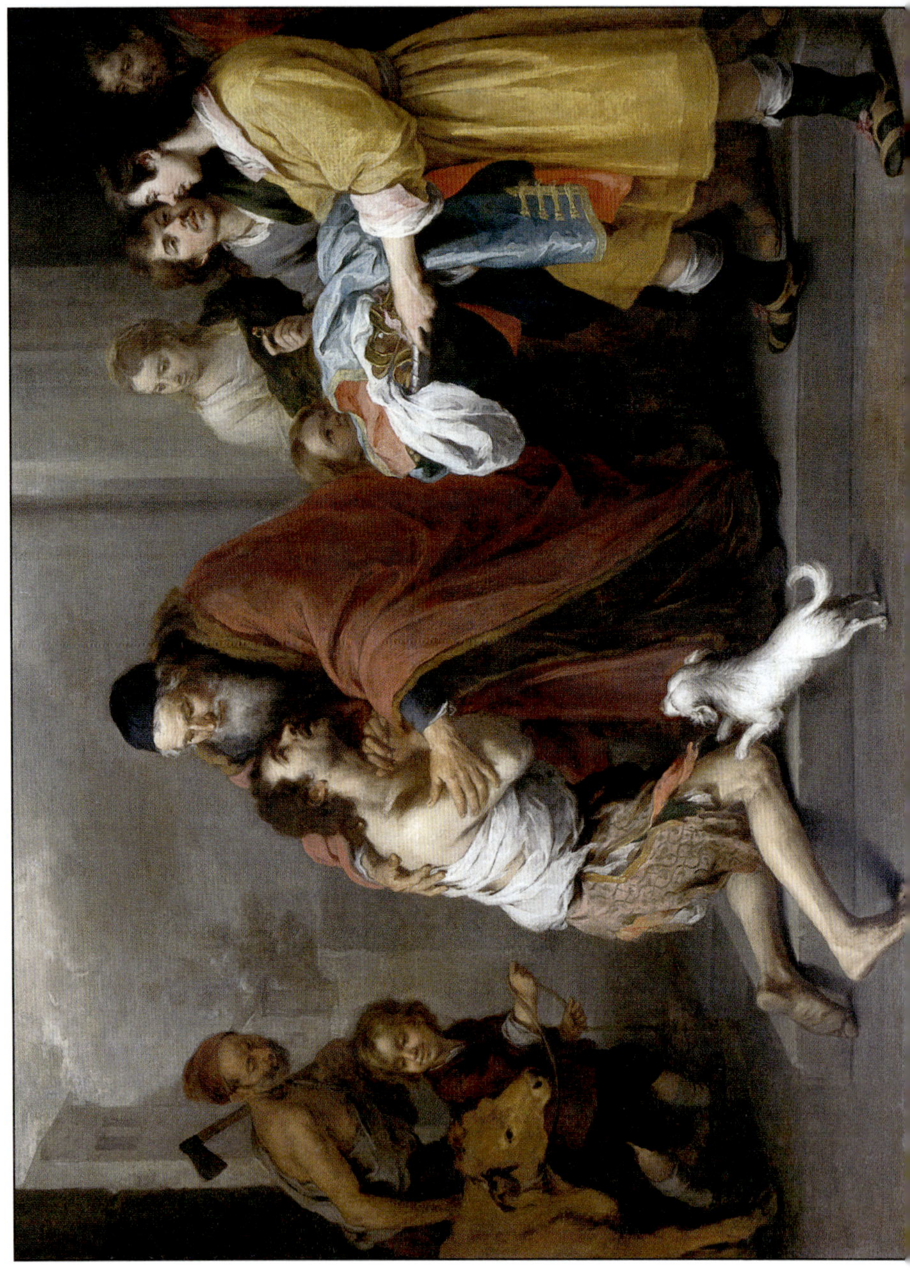

2

The Return of the Prodigal Son

The greatest teacher who ever walked the earth used parables as His primary teaching tool, stories that included images and social dynamics readily familiar to His audience. That is why He spoke often of sheep and shepherds, wedding feasts, sowing seeds, and winepresses. Among many parables that Jesus used, the Parable of the prodigal son (alternatively known as the parable of two sons or the parable of the loving father) is one of the most beloved (see Luke 15:11–32).

This parable illustrates so well the dynamics of the Christian spiritual life. It illuminates the human condition before God, and it provides hope that our past decisions, even the worst of them, are not the end of the story. It incites in us a desire for conversion and, often, it is an agent of grace that helps us decide to turn away from the "far country" of sin and toward our loving Father.

Throughout the history of Christian art, many artists have depicted this parable. While all are worthy of meditation, and while each captures some deep and unique aspects of the parable, Bartolome Esteban Murillo's rendition of *The Return of the Prodigal Son*, painted in the late 1660s, is eminent among them for capturing so many of the parable's themes and details.[20]

The focal point of Murillo's masterpiece is the moment when the father embraces the son and calls for the celebration. The biblical narrative tells us about the son's initial rejection of his patrimony, the psychological and spiritual wretchedness of the "far country" into which he traveled, and the "reckless living" in which he engaged (Luke 15:13, ESV), and the artist captures these details in the son's appearance: he wears tattered rags for clothes, and his feet are dirty, indicating not only that he did not have shoes for the long journey but also the unclean condition of his spirit. His hands are clasped in a posture of prayer as he begs forgiveness. We can nearly hear the words that St. Luke's Gospel places on his lips: "Father, I have sinned against heaven and against you; I no longer deserve to be called your son" (Luke 15:21). The son's gesture, and recalling his words in the Bible, points the viewer directly toward the Sacrament of Reconciliation, wherein we confess, with this son, our offenses against the Heavenly Father.

How do I see my own story in the younger son's? How long has it been since I have been to Reconciliation? How frequently do I access the Father's infinite mercy in Confession? Do I approach that sacrament understanding that I have wandered into a "far country" and "reckless living"?

[20] *The Return of the Prodigal Son*, by Bartolomé Esteban Murillo, can be found at the National Gallery of Art in Washington D.C.

At the father's left hand are the servants to whom he gave swift and adamant instruction. They carry the robe, the ring, and the shoes that identify the son as a beloved, privileged member of this household. To the father's right, we see the fattened calf, ready to be slaughtered for the feast by a servant wielding a butcher's tool (see Luke 15:22–23). Do I see myself as a privileged member of the Heavenly Father's household? Do I realize that He desires to shower lavish gifts upon me, despite my unworthiness? Perhaps more importantly, do I realize that the Father intends the same for others?

The scene also includes some others, a woman and two children, surrounding the father and son and servants. This reminds us that the father had called for a celebration, a feast (see Luke 15:24). Surely the celebration included the whole household, including other servants. Murillo's inclusion of this detail reminds each of us that we get to celebrate with the Father regardless of our social or economic condition. Have I participated in celebrating another person's significant conversion, rejoicing in the Heavenly Father's mercy and generosity?

Finally, we must consider the older son in the parable. Is he painted into the scene? With great artistic skill, Murillo allows the viewer to consider this older son from at least two vantage points. At the right-hand edge of the painting is a figure shrouded in darkness. It seems that this is Murillo's depiction of the older son who refused to go to the celebration. Yet Murillo also may have intended one of the characters in the foreground to convey the older son's bitterness. The character who picks up the ring bears a look on his face that almost seems to question, "You mean *he* gets to wear *this*?" This character in the parable often seems to capture our attention, because all of us know that we are like that older son, not quite ready to forgive and embrace and celebrate. We often express bitterness about the graces that other people receive.

Has there been a time when I have refused to see and accept God's merciful love for another person? Has it been because I thought that person unworthy? Because I wanted my idea of justice to prevail? Have I shrouded myself in spiritual darkness by feeling entitled or by thinking judgmentally about someone's past?

The parable of the prodigal son has such enduring power because it shines an uncomfortable light on our own minds and souls. Murillo's masterpiece elicits a host of deep, spiritual questions that, when taken along with the biblical passage, illuminates the viewer's psychological and spiritual status. All of us will do well to gaze upon it and ponder how God desires to redeem us in spite of our spiritual imperfections and depraved choices.

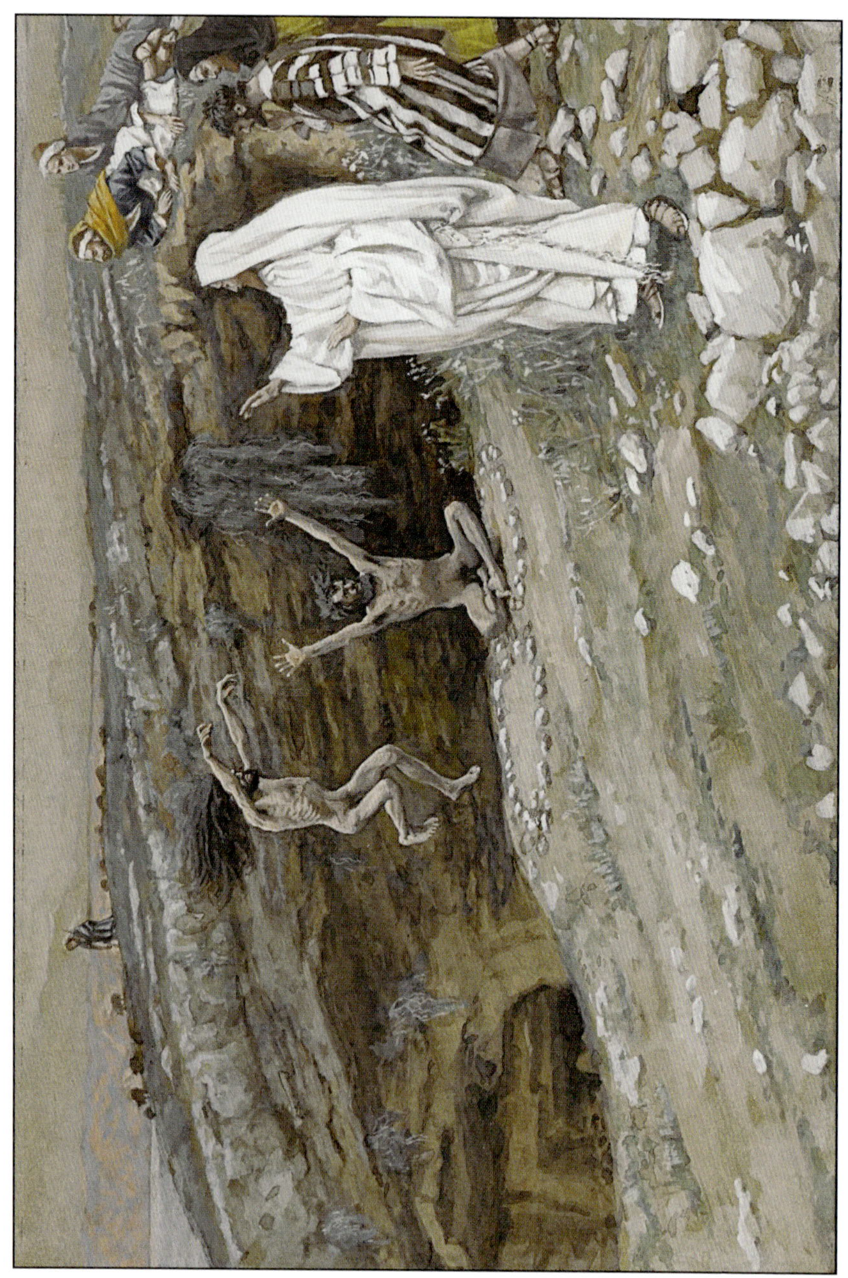

3

Two Men Possessed with Devils

As He taught about the moral and spiritual life, Jesus also traveled around curing illnesses and deformities and casting out demons. His first recorded healings and exorcisms, at least in St. Matthew's Gospel, happened in Capernaum (see Matt. 8:1–17). From Capernaum, Jesus entered a boat on the Sea of Galilee and brought "great calm" to the wind and the waves in the midst of a storm (see Matt. 8:23–27). Then, on that eastern shore of the sea, somewhere near the Decapolis, Jesus entered "the territory of the Gadarenes," healed two demoniacs, and sent a heard of swine barreling quickly into the sea (see Matt. 8:28–34).

This story of the Gadarene demoniacs is one of the most startling in all the Gospel narratives, and Jacques Tissot's painting of the event is no less shocking. Tissot was a late-nineteenth-century French artist, and he painted many scenes from the Gospels throughout his career. In *Two Men Possessed with Devils*, from the early 1890s, he invites viewers to visualize this moment in Jesus' public ministry and to apply its lessons to their own daily lives.

Jesus is in the foreground of the scene, dressed totally in white. Clearly, the artist meant for His clothing to signify His purity and perfection, especially in contrast to the demon-possessed men at the center of the scene. His right arm and hand are raised in the posture of casting out evil spirits and providing a blessing. Those of us who long to be better disciples of the Lord must ask a probing question here: Do I hold fast to the conviction that Jesus is both pure and powerful at all times? Do I believe that He can share that purity and power with me to change and strengthen my life? Ultimately, each of us has sinful tendencies or attachments that need to be cast out from our lives and that we are incapable of casting out fully without the grace and help of Our Blessed Lord.

Jesus' attention is directly on the two demoniacs, who are completely naked and unkempt and who are making wild gestures toward the Son of God and the few curious bystanders. We can almost hear their question, recorded by St. Matthew: "What have you to do with us, Son of God? Have you come here to torment us before the appointed time?" (Matt. 8:29). These men and their reaction provide an important window into our own spiritual lives. While we may not be possessed by demons, we certainly find ourselves under attack by the enemy and his minions. These attacks are best combatted by the sacraments, a deep and abiding prayer life, and a robust understanding of the moral principles given by Jesus and the Church. Each of us should also ask ourselves if there are patterns in our lives that cause us to be spiritually disheveled or filthy. What are our reactions when the grace and power of God come up against our sinful tendencies? Do we lash out in pride or envy or anger, tormented by the Lord's light and love?

Tissot depicts a few curious bystanders near Jesus and the demoniacs. These must be the local citizens who would not even enter this vicinity because these two demoniacs were "so savage" (Matt. 8:28). We notice immediately, though, that Jesus stands between them and the dangerous men. A couple lounges on the grass. They look curiously at the rocky cleft where the tombs resided and watch the possessed men. Another man looks like he is ready to move closer to the demoniacs. As we ponder this scene, we should reflect on moments when we have found courage to say or do something, with Jesus Christ as our shield and sword, that we could not say or do previously.

On the other side of the cleft, at the top left of the scene, stands a shepherd with the "herd of many pigs" that was "feeding at some distance" from the main characters of the scene. When the demons asked Our Lord to be sent into the herd of swine, Jesus commanded, "Go then!" (Matt. 8:30–32). The reaction of the herdsmen was to flee into the nearby town, where "they reported everything" (Matt. 8:33). What is our reaction to the miracles we see Our Blessed Lord working in our vicinity? Do I doubt? Am I cynical? Do I simply keep quiet? Or do I freely share with others about the amazing things I have witnessed?

Although it is not explicitly depicted by Tissot, the response of the townspeople is also important for a moment's reflection: "the whole town came out to meet Jesus" (Matt. 8:34). If the passage ended there, we might think that people coming out to meet the Miracle Worker was a normal reaction to such a show of miraculous might. Yet the narrative continues: "and when they saw him they begged him to leave their district" (Matt. 8:34). This reaction ought to cause each of us to pause and ponder. Am I afraid of letting Jesus come closer to work more miracles? Would I prefer to handle things myself, even if it means that the status quo remains? Has there ever been a time that I have rejected Jesus' offer to be present and provide healing?

Tissot's depiction of this biblical event allows us to reflect on what influences and controls us. It also invites us to ask how we might overcome that influence and reminds us that we have no power to control things on our own. Finally, we have the opportunity to ponder Jesus' position in our lives and consider whether we are ready and able to courageously share with others what Our Blessed Lord has so graciously and powerfully done for us.

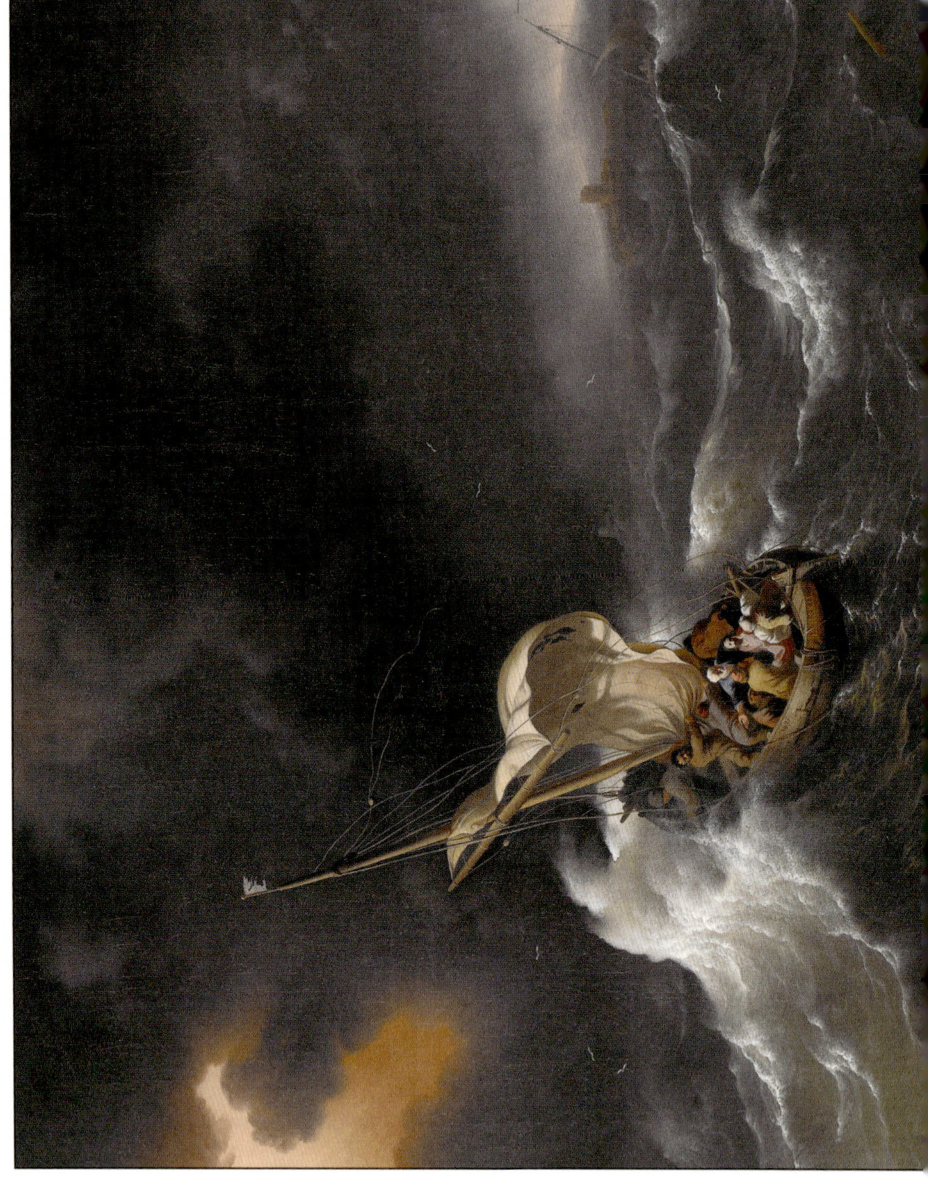

4

Christ in the Storm on the Sea of Galilee

One of the most amazing miracles Jesus performed during His public ministry was to calm the torrential storm on the Sea of Galilee (see Matt. 8:23–27; Mark 4:35–41; Luke 8:22–25). Each of the first three Gospel authors recounts the event in an effort to convey Jesus' power over all nature. Pondering this episode along with a piece of sacred art inspires readers and viewers to be amazed at Jesus' power, just as the apostles in the boat were.

Ludolf Bakhuizen (also spelled Backhuysen) was a Dutch artist of the Baroque period, known for his paintings of maritime subjects. In 1695, he completed a well-known rendition of this biblical event, titled *Christ in the Storm on the Sea of Galilee.*[21] The artist's depiction contains quite a few details that highlight the moral and spiritual truths of this moment.

[21] *Christ in the Storm on the Sea of Galilee*, by Ludolf Bakhuizen, is on display at the Indianapolis Museum of Art at Newfields.

As the viewer approaches this painting, the very first detail he or she notices is the dark clouds and stormy sea enveloping the scene. This dark storm has deep spiritual symbolism, and the viewer can identify this backdrop with his or her own temptations, traumas, and tragedies. What storm brewing, current or from my past, must I navigate?

Piercing through the darkness on either side of the painting are small shafts of light. The light from the left edge falls on the painting's largest wave, which is about to overcome the central object, the boat carrying Jesus and these apostles. The artist's use of light in this way illuminates at least two important truths of the Christian life. First, we are able to see problems best with the aid of divine illumination. The Christian is not to think that problems do not exist but, rather, to view the problems of history and society and our own interior psychology in light of the truth that God has revealed. Second, it gives visual expression to the Christian virtue of hope: even with portentous storms creating a disruption, there is still hope that peace will eventually be regained.

There are other signs of distress for this boat and crew. The boat's sail is torn slightly, and it is untethered from some of the ropes that connect it to the mast. The standard atop the mast is completely torn, almost gone totally. These images can be considered both historically and personally. The artist painted this piece, and his other most notable works, at the end of the seventeenth century. At that point, Europe had recently been torn asunder by the wars of religion that waged throughout the continent in the wake of the Protestant Reformation. Perhaps more importantly, this painting was produced at the beginning of the Enlightenment and the Scientific Revolution, both of which effectively untethered mankind from his nature as a creature of God, the omniscient and omnipotent divine reality. These images can also incite reflection on the ways that our personal lives have become detached from the secure divine pillar and tattered by life's travails.

The shaft of light from the left side of the painting makes the traveling crew the most visible portion of the scene. Nine figures occupy the barque, including Jesus. Four work to stabilize the boat, drawing in the sail while the others wake Jesus. Of this last group, one lifts the Master's head, one kneels in supplication, and one points to the wave that could destroy the ship, leaving passengers for dead. The viewer can almost hear the sailors calling out for rescue and salvation: "Teacher, do you not care that we are perishing?" (Mark 4:38). The artist has highlighted this dynamic as a constant struggle of the moral and spiritual life. Each of us has experienced travails, physically or emotionally or morally, to the point of needing to call out for help. Have I been able to recognize the specific troubles that have unmoored me from my Savior? Do I trust that Jesus desires to mend my life and bring me securely into the eternal embrace of the Trinity?

At the right-hand edge of the painting, the viewer notices another boat struggling against the wind and waves. This boat is present in order to visualize the fact, recorded by St. Mark, that "other boats were with him" (Mark 4:36). In that boat, we see no more than a few sailors, but we also see that their sail and standard are fully intact. Behind the second ship is a landmass marked by what seems to be a broken column or tree. One boat in the scene seems headed toward the land; the other boat seems oriented away. Behind the landmass is the other source of light in the scene, reminding the viewer of the truth taught by St. Paul that "the church of the living God [is] the pillar and bulwark of the truth" (1 Tim. 3:15, RSVCE).

These details illuminate some of the most significant realities of the moral and spiritual life: What are the stable foundations in my life? Have storms ensued as I have left those foundations? Do I seek the solid foundation of Jesus and the Church in the midst of life's storms?

Finally, seven white birds fly around the scene. What might these birds signify? The most significant lists of seven that come readily to mind are the seven sacraments and the seven Gifts of the Holy Spirit. Just as birds are not affected by maritime storms in the same ways as sailors, neither are Christian disciples affected by the buffets of life when they rely on these grace-filled provisions of God. God has already provided the tools and gifts we need to traverse the dark, perilous ocean of modern culture and to arrive surely and safely to our heavenly homeland. Have I developed a deep and ongoing devotion to the sacraments of the Church? How can I access the Gifts of the Holy Spirit more effectively?

Visualizing these important spiritual truths is the rich gift that the viewer finds in Bakhuizen's masterpiece. The artist has deftly employed artistic technique and style, along with his signature maritime motif, to allow the viewer to connect this biblical episode to his or her own life.

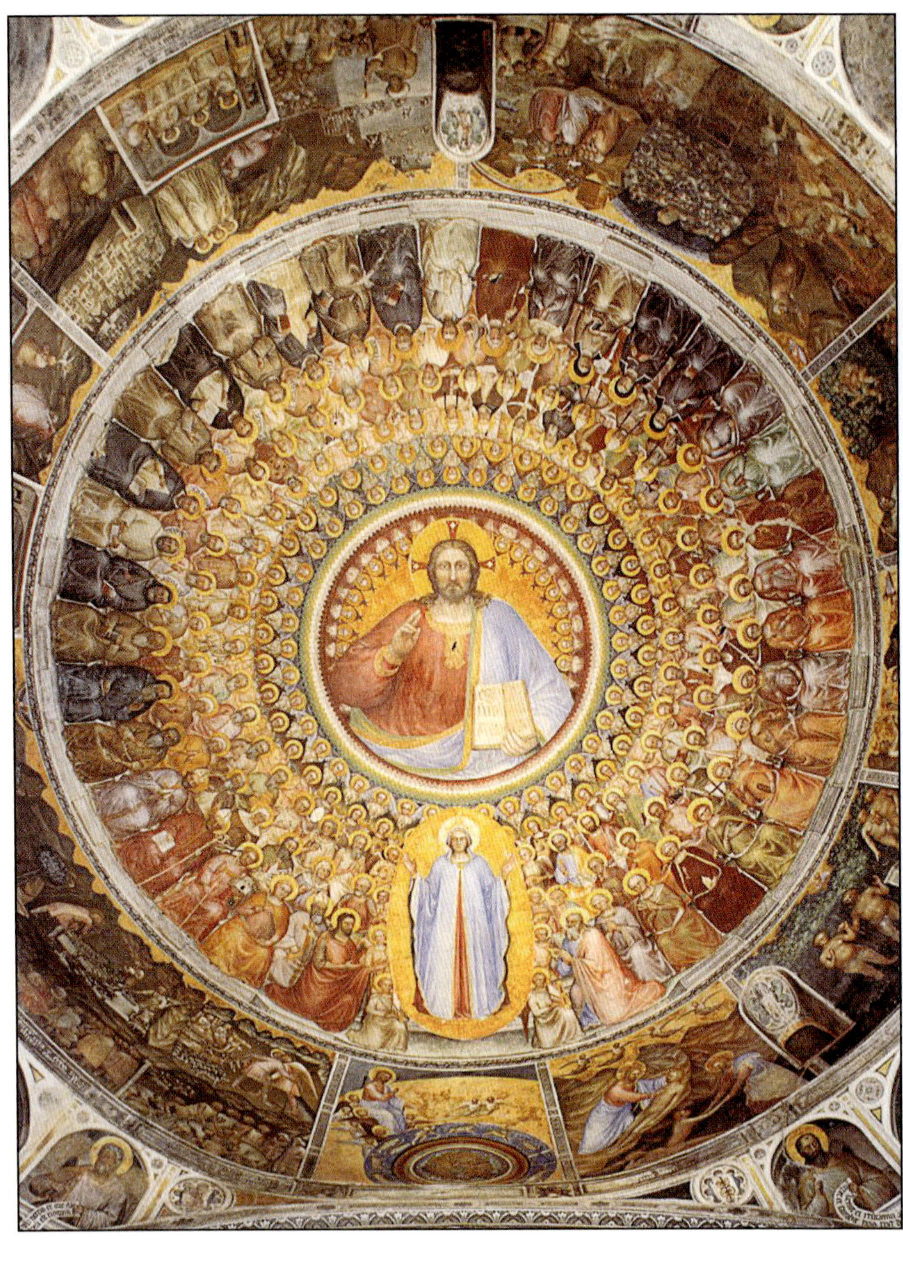

Epilogue: Paradise

THE GRACED TASK of the essays in this book has been to ponder the unfolding mystery of salvation and redemption through sacred art. We began with the expectation of the advent of the Messiah. We have meditated on Our Blessed Lord's Nativity and childhood and quiet years in Nazareth. We have gazed deeply on some of the most memorable moments of His public ministry. We have pondered how suffering and sacrifice lead through the Cross to the full completion of redemption. Now, it is appropriate to conclude our study of praying through sacred art by reflecting on the destination each of us desires and seeks by living in God's grace: the everlasting Kingdom of Heaven.

In the Middle Ages, Christendom was the name given to the all-pervasive culture placed under the divine lordship of Jesus Christ. All things, including art and architecture, were ordered toward drawing individuals and communities into the communion of saints. Much more than our own, that culture knew that the things of this world point us toward, and culminate in, the eternal paradise.

The baptistry of the Cathedral of St. John the Baptist in Padua, Italy, expresses this reality well. While the structure was built at least a century before, the art within was crafted by Giusto de' Menabuoi from 1375 to 1378, at the zenith of the High Middle Ages. The entirety of this baptistry and the visual art within provides the viewer with a much deeper appreciation of the way that sacred art brings us into the mystery of salvation, into the work of Jesus and the Church that leads humanity to its redemption.

First, we must consider the purpose of the structure itself. In the Middle Ages, a baptistry was used as an antechamber to accessing the rest of the Church's treasures, her sacramental life, her work, and her devotions. We recall that Baptism, and all the sacramental life in its wake, is at the core of the Church's mission. Jesus clearly taught that "unless one is born of water and the Spirit, he cannot enter the kingdom of God" (John 3:5, ESV), and He commissioned His apostles, "Go, therefore, and make disciples of all nations, baptizing them" (Matt. 28:19).

But Jesus did not conclude His commission there. He went further: "teaching them to observe all that I have commanded you" (Matt. 28:20). Thus, we realize that teaching is also at the core of the Church's mission. Before the printing press and widespread literacy, teaching happened through art. Therefore, the frescoes on the walls of the baptistry are a gift that unfold the whole story of salvation from the creation of the world through the mission and ministry of the Church. These frescoes have therefore helped Christians throughout history extend the work of Jesus.

We know, then, that this structure is iconic of what the Lord intends for His Chosen People, specifically through the sacrament of Baptism. Have I recognized the power of my own Baptism? Have I understood that my Baptism grants a purpose and a mission to me? Have I celebrated my Baptism? Am I inspired by the fact that my Baptism incorporates me into the Church and Her mission? What gifts do I have to share the Good News of salvation with others?

Inside the baptistry, frescoes cover every wall, seemingly every crevice. Many of them depict the earthly lives of St. John the Baptist and Jesus. Others intentionally connect biblical events to the ongoing life of the Church. There is a smaller dome above the baptistry's altar that portrays the descent of the Holy Spirit at Pentecost, inviting the viewer to recall the biblical event that gave birth to the Church's mission in the world. The frescoed walls around the altar show images and scenes from the Apocalypse of St. John (that is, the book of Revelation), reminding us that the final book of the Bible puts the mystical vision of the heavenly liturgy into words. Without a doubt, the art here is both overwhelming and inspiring.

All of the surrounding art, though, is intended to draw the viewer's eyes upward into the central dome. The base of that dome includes depictions of thirty-three episodes from Genesis. The cycle begins with the creation of the world and concludes with the story of Jacob wrestling with God. Quite possibly, the author intended to tell the story of God's covenant people struggling to remain faithful after Original Sin. How has sin caused a deep wound in my life? Has my struggle with sin limited my ability to remain in covenant relationship with God?

Higher up the central dome is the main fresco, simply titled *Paradise*. This fresco is an icon pointing out that all the teaching and sacramental ministry of the Church leads to the establishment of the eternal Kingdom. Do I realize that every part of life, the joyful celebrations and the vicissitudes and the sacrifices, are ways that God can bring me closer to eternal life with Him? Do I desire to live eternally in Paradise?

The arrangement of the painted figures around the dome is also instructive. Directly above the main entrance to the baptistry, and above the fresco depicting creation, is an image of the Virgin Mary, clad in blue and surrounded by a mandorla of flame. This is a visual expression of the Catholic teaching that Mary's *fiat* facilitated the new creation made effective in Jesus Christ. She is much larger than the other saints whose images fill the dome. All these details indicate the importance of devotion to the Blessed Mother during the course of our efforts to grow in full relationship with Jesus, her Divine Son. Do I have a relationship with Mary? Do I have a devotion to Jesus' Mother? Do I ask her to take me to her Son and allow me to be made new?

Around the dome, in layers ascending toward the apex, a plethora of saints are depicted from every facet of the Church's life. Some are bishops and some are deacons. Some hold books, indicating the importance of the intellectual life, while others play musical instruments, indicating the range of Christian devotions. Some are clearly Dominicans while others are obviously Franciscans, and still others are from various other religious communities. Some wear tiaras, indicating nobility, and others wield walking staffs, indicating a more mendicant lifestyle. Still, no matter the particular expression, all of these men and women wear the halo of sanctity, the imperishable crown for which they cultivated heroic virtue during their earthly life (see 1 Cor. 9:24–27). This is a visual expression of the communion of saints, which is intended to include everyone from every part of the world and from every part of the social order. Are there particular saints whose examples can inspire me in my journey toward Paradise? Do I ask for their intercession frequently?

The center of the dome is occupied by an image of Christ Pantocrator ("Ruler of All"). In His left hand, Jesus holds a book. The page on the left side is discernible to the viewer and, in Greek, reads, "Ego sum A ω" ("I am the Alpha and Omega" in English; see Rev. 22:13). These details remind us of Jesus' role as the just and merciful Judge at the culmination of human history. Specifically, we are reminded of St. Paul's words to the Corinthians: "When everything is subjected to him, then the Son himself will [also] be subjected to the one who subjected everything to him, so that God may be all in all" (1 Cor. 15:28; see also CCC 671 and 679).

Each of the frescoes painted by Menabuoi in this baptistry inspire in the viewer a desire to know more about salvation history and the One who fulfills all the previous covenants. More importantly, the layout of the art on the walls, leading upward into the central dome, is meant to cause each viewer to desire to be inserted into the concentric circles of holy men and women who worship the Triumphant Christ in Heaven for all eternity.

This idea, ultimately, has been the aim of this series of prayerful meditations using *visio divina*. Prayer with sacred art ought to inspire each of us to seek a deeper connection to Jesus and the Church so that we may receive the manifold blessings that Our Blessed Lord offers to us. Prayer with sacred art also ought to impel us to carry His grace and truth into the settings of our everyday lives. Meditating on these images allows us to build up a mystical art museum in our minds and hearts by which we can remain connected to Him unto the fulfillment of our lives, and by which we can invite others to join us.

Image Credits

The Eve of the Deluge by William Bell Scott, Tate Britain, London, Public Domain, commons.wikimedia.org

St. John the Baptist Preaching by Mattia Preti, Fine Arts Museums of San Francisco, California, Public Domain, commons.wikimedia.org

St John the Baptist in the Prison by Juan Fernández de Navarrete, Hermitage Museum, St. Petersburg, Public Domain, commons.wikimedia.org

The Dream of Saint Joseph by Francisco Goya, Saragossa Museum, Spain, Public Domain, commons.wikimedia.org

The Annunciation by Henry Ossawa Tanner, Philadelphia Museum of Art, Philadelphia, Public Domain, commons.wikimedia.org

The Meeting of Mary and Elisabeth by Carl Heinrich Bloch, Frederiksborg Castle, (P5H0BD) The Picture Art Collection / Alamy.com

Adoration of the Shepherds by Gerard van Honthorst, Pomeranian State Museum, Western Pomerania, Public Domain, commons.wikimedia.org

The Adoration of the Magi by Peter Paul Rubens, Museo del Prado, Madrid, Public Domain, commons.wikimedia.org.

Simeon and Anna in the Temple by Rembrandt van Rijn, Hamburger Kunsthalle, Hamburg, Public Domain, commons.wikimedia.org

Holy Family in the Carpentry Shop by Gerrit van Honthorst, Museum & Gallery, Bob Jones University, South Carolina, (SSI2202230), Superstock / Bridgeman Images

Christ Among the Doctors by Philippe de Champaigne, Musée des Beaux-Arts, Angers, Public Domain, commons.wikimedia.org

Temptation of Christ by Philips Augustijn Immenraet, Museum of John Paul II Collection, Warsaw, Public Domain, commons.wikimedia.org

Transfiguration by Theophanes the Greek, Tretyakov Gallery, Moscow, (2JB2B37) CBW / Alamy.com

Christ and the Samaritan Woman by Lavinia Fontana, Museo di Capodimonte, Naples, (2AGRJ5N) Album / Alamy.com

Healing of the Man Born Blind by Orazio de Ferrari, Collection of the Banca Carige, Genoa, Public Domain, commons.wikimedia.org

The Raising of Lazarus by Caravaggio, Museo Regionale, Messina, Sicily, Public Domain, commons.wikimedia.org

The Institution of the Eucharist during the Last Supper by Peter Paul Rubens, Pinacoteca di Brera, Milan, Public Domain, commons.wikimedia.org

The Isenheim Altarpiece by Matthias Grünewald and Nikolaus Hagenauer, Unterlinden Museum, France, Public Domain, commons.wikimedia.org

The Three Women at the Tomb of Christ by Irma Martin, Private Collection, Public Domain, commons.wikimedia.org

The Incredulity of St. Thomas by Caravaggio, Sanssouci Picture Gallery, Germany, Public Domain, commons.wikimedia.org

The Supper at Emmaus by Matthias Stom, Thyssen-Bornemisza Museum, Madrid, Public Domain, commons.wikimedia.org

The Good Shepherd by Murillo, Museo del Prado, Madrid, Public Domain, commons.wikimedia.org

Christ Pantocrator Unknown Artist, St. Catherine Monastery, Sinai, Public Domain, commons.wikimedia.org

The Ascension by Benjamin West, Denver Art Museum, Colorado, Public Domain, commons.wikimedia.org

Pentecost: The Holy Ghost Descends upon Mary and the Apostles by Anthony van Dyck, Prussian Palaces and Gardens Foundation Berlin-Brandenburg, German, Public Domain, commons.wikimedia.org

The Baptism of Christ by Peter Paul Rubens, Royal Museum of Fine Arts Antwerp, Belgium, Public Domain, commons.wikimedia.org

Christ Calling the Apostles James and John by Edward Armitage, (MPCE2C) painters / Alamy.com

The Marriage at Cana by Maerten de Vos, Onze-Lieve-Vrouwekathedraal, Belgium, Public Domain, commons.wikimedia.org

The Sermon on the Mount by Carl Bloch, The Museum of National History at Frederiksborg Castle, Denmark, Public Domain, commons.wikimedia.org

Transfiguration by Raphael, Pinacoteca Vaticana, Vatican City, Public Domain, commons.wikimedia.org

The Good Samaritan Tends the Wounds of the Wounded Traveller by Balthasar van Cortbemde, Royal Museum of Fine Arts Antwerp, Belgium, Public Domain, commons.wikimedia.org

The Return of the Prodigal Son by Murillo, National Gallery of Art, USA, Public Domain, commons.wikimedia.org

The Two Men Possessed with Devils by James Tissot, Brooklyn Museum, Brooklyn, Public Domain, commons.wikimedia.org

Christ in the Storm on the Sea of Galilee by Ludolf Bakhuizen, Indianapolis Museum of Art, Indianapolis, Public Domain, commons.wikimedia.org

Paradise by Giusto de' Menabuoi, Padua Baptistery, Padua, (JHJG81) Historic Images / Alamy.com

About the Author

DEREK ROTTY IS a freelance author who lives in Jackson, Tennessee, with his wife and five children. He holds advanced degrees in history and theology. He has written extensively on Catholic history and culture, evangelization and catechesis, and the family. Find out more about him and his work at derekrotty.com.

Sophia Institute

Sophia Institute is a nonprofit institution that seeks to nurture the spiritual, moral, and cultural life of souls and to spread the gospel of Christ in conformity with the authentic teachings of the Roman Catholic Church.

Sophia Institute Press fulfills this mission by offering translations, reprints, and new publications that afford readers a rich source of the enduring wisdom of mankind.

Sophia Institute also operates the popular online resource CatholicExchange.com. *Catholic Exchange* provides world news from a Catholic perspective as well as daily devotionals and articles that will help readers to grow in holiness and live a life consistent with the teachings of the Church.

In 2013, Sophia Institute launched Sophia Institute for Teachers to renew and rebuild Catholic culture through service to Catholic education. With the goal of nurturing the spiritual, moral, and cultural life of souls, and an abiding respect for the role and work of teachers, we strive to provide materials and programs that are at once enlightening to the mind and ennobling to the heart; faithful and complete, as well as useful and practical.

Sophia Institute gratefully recognizes the Solidarity Association for preserving and encouraging the growth of our apostolate over the course of many years. Without their generous and timely support, this book would not be in your hands.

www.SophiaInstitute.com
www.CatholicExchange.com
www.SophiaTeachers.org